JOSEPH ALLAMANO
Founder of the Consolata Missionaries

D1491038

DOMENICO AGASSO

JOSEPH ALLAMANO
Founder of the Consolata Missionaries

Translated by Alan Neame

Published by
ST PAUL PUBLICATIONS
for
ISTITUTO MISSIONI CONSOLATA

Original Title: *Fare bene il bene. Giuseppe Allamano*
© 1990 Edizioni Paoline s.r.l., Cinisello Balsamo, Italy

English language edition published for
Istituto Missioni Consolata
Viale delle Mura Aurelie 11-13, 00165 Roma, Italy
by
St Paul Publications
Middlegreen, Slough SL3 6BT, United Kingdom

© 1991 Istituto Missioni Consolata, Roma

ISBN 085439 386 2

Printed by Billings, Worcester

Contents

Guide to the use of the word 'Consolata'

The Consolata Missionary Institute was founded in 1901 by Fr Joseph Allamano. Its Mother House is in Turin.

The Consolata Missionaries are priests, brothers and sisters.

Consolatina is the name given to the Consolata Missionaries' first house in Turin.

The Consolata is the monthly magazine published by the Consolata Missionary Institute.

Consolata is the Italian name for Our Lady of Consolation, from whom the Institute takes its name. The same name is used to denote:

- Our Lady of Consolation
- The Shrine of Our Lady of Consolation in Turin
- The Missionary Institute founded by Fr Allamano
- The Mother House of the Missionary Institute

Preface

In truth, the 'procession of saints', where Turin is concerned, knows no end. In May 1990 two more were added to it: Fr Filippo Rinaldi, a Salesian priest, and Pier Giorgio Frassati, a young layman. Then, in October, there was a third addition: Fr Joseph Allamano, a diocesan priest. There are others too on the waiting list, many of them, of every type, to show how many-coloured and beautiful is the wedding garment of Christ's bride, the Church, all glorious, 'without spot or wrinkle or any such thing, but holy and without blemish' (Eph 5:27).

Writing the life of a saint cannot be easy. But that it may be enthralling cannot be denied. Writing any biography is hard. By nature, writing fixes, imposes limits, schematizes. Life is infinitely richer than what can be pinned down and fixed on paper. Even when, in the writing, the subject is set in its historical context and enriched by perspicacity and extensive thought. But for the saints it is more difficult still.

Grace and history interlace and are constantly interacting one on the other: if the latter can be described and classified by dates and places, the former is like hidden sap, to be discovered by degrees and manifesting itself in its fruit. Eyes of sight for consulting the documents are not enough; the eyes of the heart are needed, of a believing heart. For holiness, the fruit of grace, is the history of individual faith.

In producing a new biography of Fr Joseph Allamano, Domenico Agasso is thoroughly familiar with the sources, beginning with Tubaldo's two thick volumes; at the same time he has the skill to investigate the secret source, the gifts of God. The interaction is constant in each chapter. With essential but sure brush strokes, a clear and telling style, he sites Allamano's development in the historical and religious context of his times, reconstructing with rare authenticity what life was like in the seminary, at the Consolata, at the Pastoral Institute (the *Convitto Ecclesiastico*),

1

in the diocese, in the world of Piedmont and in the universal Church itself.

With balance and discretion he then brings out the design
of the spiritual quality of those virtues cultivated with un-
wavering fidelity by this learned and bashful priest: who was
patient and decisive, exact and authoritarian, obedient and
prophetic, orderly in study and in life, physically frail and
tirelessly creative of works and foundations. Never moving outside Turin, and staying for years and years, more
than forty, until the end of his life, in his first post as rector of the Consolata and the Pastoral Institute, he
reconstructed, enlarged and embellished the Shrine and
founded and governed the Consolata Missionary Fathers
and the Consolata Missionary Sisters. With his 'soft voice'
he managed to reach all the Churches of Italy through their
bishops, up to the Pope himself, pleading that he, with his
apostolic authority, would proclaim the mission of
evangelization to all nations as a duty, and institute a Mission Sunday to be observed year by year 'with the obligation of a sermon on the duty and methods of propagating
the faith throughout the world'.

Of course, Allamano was also heir to a spiritual tradition which, in the course of four wars ending with the first
of this century, sadly known as 'Great', gave birth to a list
of saints to be numbered by the dozen, and notably those
most closely connected with him: John Bosco, Joseph Cottolengo and above all his own uncle Joseph Cafasso. He
was debtor too to Turin's great missionary century, for there
it was that the Work of the Propagation of the Faith, started
in France, was set up as early as 1824, and that Canon
Giuseppe Ortalda published his periodical *Museo delle
Missioni Cattoliche*, which was Italy's first missionary
magazine.

In the Church, no one is an absolute innovator. Christ
alone is that. Each saint — and we are each called to be
one and ought, each of us, want to become one — is and
is aware of being a child of the Church, and aware, because
of this, of having to give everything to the Church. To regard
himself, even if unconsciously, as the starter of everything
and as it were among 'the founding or re-founding fathers'
was never Allamano's attitude. He had a deep and living

2

sense of the Church, bound to its bishops, to an unbroken continuity, immersed in a sacred history.

On this score, two points warrant emphasizing.

As a diocesan priest, the trainer of secular priests, a canon of the cathedral, present and active in every one of the diocese's spiritual, charitable and social undertakings, from Catholic newspapers to working-men's clubs, Allamano exhibited a missionary awareness in the Church as it existed in Turin, such as it should be universal throughout the Catholic Church, since 'mission' is the Church's identity and hence the condition on which the Church's vitality depends.

Precisely because he loves Jesus in the Eucharist and serves him in his priestly ministry, he knows he can allow himself no rest until this bread of heaven is broken for the hunger of the whole human race, the hunger for eternal life. For Christians, feeding the hungry is the first of the works of mercy, because they know everyone hungers for resurrection since all have been created and predestined in Christ crucified and risen.

Precisely because he loves the Blessed Virgin Mary and serves her, sparing no expense to make her symbolic dwelling in Turin as beautiful as he can, he understands that all humanity needs a 'consoling evangelization', allowing all to meet today everywhere on earth and see the Son of Mary, the only Saviour, the Father of all consolation's Consolation made visible, and with him his mother: Mary, Our Lady of Consolation.

Long before Vatican II, Allamano was already persuaded of what was to be declared in the decree *Presbyterorum Ordinis*: 'The spiritual gift which priests receive at their ordination prepares them not for any limited and narrow mission but for the widest scope of the universal mission of salvation "even to the very ends of the earth". For every priestly ministry shares in the universality of the mission entrusted by Christ to his apostles' (PO 10), and 'their life has also been consecrated to the service of the missions' (AG 39).

The other point to be emphasized concerns the relationship between Allamano's missionary activity and the local Church. As the founder of two missionary institutes, he still wished to remain an ordinary diocesan priest and wanted to do nothing without the approval of his bishops; hence he had the biblical patience to say nothing and wait for a long time. He only begins when his bishop, Agostino Richelmy, says to him, 'Yes, the Institute must be founded and you are the man to do it' and, again, before proceeding to the foundation, he asks the opinion and obtains the approval of all the bishops in Piedmont. His missionaries do not set out in his name but as envoys of their Church.

Emblematic of this is the gesture of Archbishop Richelmy who — as is related here — receives the four departing missionaries, 'arranges to be left alone with them, makes them sit side by side and then kneels down to kiss their feet.' The feet that trod the streets of the world to bring the tidings of the Gospel would never have been able to forget their Church of origin.

The community of believers in Christ is, as it were, brought about by the network of missions which all have as origin the saving initiative of the Father, whose will is that all should be saved. Wherever they arrive, they plant the Church and whoever preaches the Gospel associates himself or herself with whoever accepts it, making that person jointly responsible, thus gradually bringing its catechists to birth and next its priests and then its bishops, so whoever gives receives, and who receives gives, or — to put it in the polished words of this biography — 'every baptism, rather than being a victory for the missionary, will be the sanction of a common conquest, of the one who has set forth the faith and the one who has accepted it. If at the end of the twentieth century there are vigorous local Churches with their own pastors, flourishing in this territory, the reason why is hidden in the years of sowing at the beginning of the century, in the joint work of the missionaries on site and the rector piloting them from Turin, in the shadow of the Consolata.'

All this being so, it is a significant fact that the Pope was pleased to beatify the priest, Canon Joseph Allamano, precisely on 7 October 1990, the first Sunday of Missions Month, during the Synod of Bishops on the training of priests.

Allamano's biography can give us readers incomparable light and support in helping us to recover 'the fair image of the priest', rekindle enthusiasm for high apostolic ideals in the

4

young and keep missionary awareness and co-operation alive among the whole people of God.

Each saint's story is always a living commentary on the unique Gospel for a specific time and for the needs of the Church. So we ought to start reading the lives of the saints once more. They represent a grace not to be neglected. And I hope that this biography of our new Blessed, Joseph Allamano, which reads as a thrilling spiritual adventure, may become widely known, to priests and laity and to young people in particular. I am sure that much can come of this encounter. Hence I have no hesitation in urging the young to read it.

GIOVANNI SALDARINI
Archbishop of Turin

1
The rugged hills

In the parish church of Castelnuovo d'Asti a new priest was celebrating his First Mass, on the feast of Our Lady of Sorrows, Sunday 21 September 1873. His name was Joseph Allamano, turned twenty-two in January. He had been ordained to the priesthood in Turin Cathedral by Archbishop Gastaldi the previous day, Saturday 20 September, the third anniversary of the fall of Rome. In the capital the anniversary had been marked in two ways, which were to become traditional: at the Porta Pia, processions, flags and antipapal speeches; in the Vatican, protests by the Pontiff. This year Pius IX described to the Black Aristocracy what his state of mind had been, that 20 September 1870, after listening briefly to the thunder of the Italian artillery: 'Those cannonades struck me as such an excess of childish impiety that all I could think of doing was to close the window and, turning to the crucifix, exclaim, "Lord, open the window of these people's hearts and convert them. . ." '

No echo of the Roman Question reached the church in Castelnuovo. The sermon was preached by Fr Giovanni Allamano, the young celebrant's paternal uncle and provost of the near-by parish of Passerano. He spoke mainly about the great services that every good priest can render to society.

After the Mass there would normally have been a family and parish party with a big spread and a large number of guests. But Fr Joseph did not care for such things. He was never to like them. And furthermore there was a decisive argument: Archbishop Gastaldi had recently issued strict instructions on the subject: '*Epularum adparatus . . . removeas*', in other words, no sumptuous banquets and rowdy company round new priests. So lunch was served in the parish priest's house to a very small number: the local priests and Fr Joseph's brothers, that was all. Later though the brothers managed to have a small party at home, but without any offence to austerity: a reception, the recitation of one or two poems but nothing else.

This simplicity matched Fr Joseph's temperament. He was a young man of restrained behaviour and never much at ease in crowds or noise. He was an elegant and cordial conversationalist but no orator; in the pulpit he was never to shine at 'sacred eloquence'. At this particular time, priests were constantly being counselled to keep a low profile as a salutary corrective to the unbridled self-assertiveness so harmful to men of the cloth. But there was no need to insist on this with him, reserved as he was by nature.

Besides, there seemed no special reason for making a great fuss over a First Mass, since at Castelnuovo d'Asti this was by no means anything out of the ordinary. Vocations to the priesthood were not in short supply anywhere but among these hills they seemed to have a special quality about them. Don Bosco was from Castelnuovo, and that would already have been enough. For years he used to come there in the summer at the head of his boys, with music, singing and plays; and on each visit, from Castelnuovo and the surrounding country, he would rake in bright boys to take to Valdocco. Among those he had captured here was Giovanni Cagliero, a peasant lad who became a priest and later a bishop and a cardinal. At the time, Don Bosco had stopped making these forays into the area; his institutes were thriving and multiplying; King Victor Emmanuel's ministers consulted him and even Pope Pius IX was asking his advice about nominating bishops to Italian sees.

Also from Castelnuovo was Mgr Giovanni Battista Bertagna, an eminent personality in the diocese, professor of Moral Theology at the Pastoral Institute in Turin, which was, as it were, the practical training school for the young clergy. Other priests too of Castelnuovo were destined to become bishops and among them Fr Rossi, the parish priest of the place.

Over all these figures of the living, however, loomed that of Fr Giuseppe Cafasso, who had died in 1860. Father and guide to generations of priests and religious, trainer of great characters, he was at home in palaces and prisons, consulted by noblemen and invoked by cut-throats. Already renown for sanctity was growing about his name, by popular acclaim. Many of his admonitions and words of advice were quoted as prophetic: 'Fr Cafasso said that would happen. . .'

The soldier and the hermit

But before him, in 1776, a namesake of his had been born in Castelnuovo d'Asti, another Giuseppe Cafasso who led an adventurous life. Initially a priest in Turin, he had joined the Jesuits in Russia where the Society survived under the Tsar (as also in Prussia) after the suppression that Pope Clement XIV had been forced to decree. With the Jesuits he went as a missionary to the Caucasus until 1820, and from there he moved into Greece where he died in 1834.

His checkered existence was linked to a most interesting moment in sub-Alpine Catholicism, as it was also to persons whom Joseph Allamano was destined to encounter during his own life, through their works, example, heredity. Cafasso the Jesuit, in fact had been Pio Brunone Lanteri's friend and with him a disciple of Fr von Diessbach: names that made history and anticipated events, yet today seem to be totally forgotten, one wonders why.

Nikolaus Albert von Diessbach (1732–1798) was a Swiss of Bern, an army officer belonging to a prominent family of Calvinists of the most rigid sort. He became a Catholic, which caused a painful breach with his relations. Not only that. As he soon became a widower, he entered the Society of Jesus which all were then competing to vilify and hunt down, the butt of every kind of accusation until the suppression of 1773. And since that was the time when thrones on the one hand and revolutions on the other seemed bent on ruining Faith and Church, the ex-soldier Jesuit determined to organize the defence — indeed the counter-attack — with the very arms and methods of the foe.

Had the secret societies of the day and Freemasonry in particular dealt Catholicism hard blows, especially by means of the anti-clerical, anti-religious press? He in his turn organized (operating in Lombardy, Piedmont, France) another network of secret societies, Christian Fellowships, staunchly committed to producing and distributing works

8

in defence of the Catholic faith. Had the *philosophes* managed to win the ear of king and emperor? Fr Diessbach took the same route, heading particularly for Vienna in the days of Leopold II and then of his son Francis II.

It was precisely while staying in that capital city that he came by his death in mysterious circumstances: 'Having credit and access to the imperial court, he met with resentment from certain people who, convinced that they have been offended by him, treacherously had him beaten by their criminal retainers; and so grave were the insults given and the thrashing received that the holy man fell ill and shortly died.' Thus Fr Pietro Gastaldi relates his end in Pio Brunone Lanteri's biography published in 1870. Actually, Fr Lanteri, originally a hermit in the Cuneese and then in 1782 a priest in Turin, had formed part, with the Jesuit Cafasso, of the group closest to Fr Diessbach. And he carried on the work, starting in 1817 the Catholic Fellowships, lay associations, no longer secret, very active in the sphere of the press.

Even before this, when Pope Pius VII was residing at Savona from 1809 to 1812 as Napoleon's prisoner, Fr Lanteri undertook a vigorous press campaign in Italy and in France in defence of the papal prerogatives. He also initiated a sort of secret service that outwitted the vigilance of the French by supplying Pius VII with information and help. When Napoleon was considering appointing bishops without reference to the Pope, it was Fr Lanteri who clandestinely provided the Prisoner of Savona with the acts of the Council of Lyon of 1274, needed for refuting the government's arguments. At a given point however the French police suspected something was going on, and Fr Lanteri was confined for three years in a house belonging to him at Bardassano, not far from Turin.

With his encouragement and advice, the Oblates of the Virgin Mary came into existence in 1816 at Carignano, Turin: a militant congregation devoted to the extremely urgent task of re-evangelization, particularly by means of popular missions and retreats. The congregation had no easy life, beginning right from its earliest years to experience opposition and intrigue emanating even from the Curia. In every see, as long as he lived, Fr Lanteri battled away for his Oblates. A new and better clergy than before: parish priests and confessors thoroughly trained to be spiritual guides; fathers and exemplars, instead of bureaucrats of the mysteries or sullen and unheeded judges: this was his whole life's dream, the problem of all his days.

An attempt was already being made in Turin to supply this need, though privately and on a small scale, by a friend and disciple of his who had also been a member of the clandestine group to help Pius VII: Luigi Maria Guala, a priest since 1799 and collegiate theologian of the University of Turin. He had informally gathered round him a few young priests for conversations in practical moral theology. But on this matter Brunone Lanteri thought big. He wanted a real, proper school for the young priests of all Piedmont, to be admitted as boarders and given regular courses of instruction, with full recognition by the civil and ecclesiastical authorities.

In 1816 he made an official request on the subject to the Archbishop on the one hand and the government on the other, asking to be given the former convent of the Friars Minor near the Church of St Francis of Assisi. He intended to entrust the new Institute to the Oblates. But precisely because of this, the application was refused: the government was opposed to the installing of any new congregations in Turin. Instead, a new request, not mentioning the oblates, met with acceptance, this time presented, with Lanteri's agreement, by Fr Guala who was, among other things, rector of the Church of St Francis. And the Pastoral Institute opened in November 1818 with its first twelve pupils. At Fr Lanteri's death, twelve years later, the institution was already well established and thriving under Fr Guala's direction. And he, an outstanding educationalist, before his death in 1848, had the good fortune to entrust the Pastoral Institute to someone who was to raise it to its highest levels of achievement: the second Giuseppe Cafasso from Castelnuovo, the future saint, who was also Joseph Allamano's uncle.

In the days of large families and abundant clergy, an uncle-priest or uncle-religious was no rarity. Consequently Joseph Allamano found on coming into the world that he had two: his mother's brother, Fr Giuseppe Cafasso, and his father's brother Fr Giovanni Allamano, of Passerano.

the most solemn vows, I would have them annulled for you to go and look after your ailing mother.' He concluded by saying, 'Be a nun at home.' And so that was what Benedetta did, dividing her time between the infants at the nursery school, her invalid family and a life of piety. Testimonies to her joyful fervour in prayer, even in advanced years and in illness, have much in common with those describing more famous examples of holiness.

For Joseph Allamano as man and priest, the kindergarten mistress did not merely personify tender childhood memories; she even became a link, a connection between him and the country people: above all the poor, to whom, in his mother's style, he sent frequent relief, distributed of course by Benedetta. But she also grew more and more important in his eyes as one of the surviving witnesses to the life of Fr Cafasso and custodian of many a memory. Each step Joseph Allamano took in his life as priest brought him nearer to the figure of his mother's extraordinary brother, increasing his need to know more thoroughly about him and in turn to make him known. Benedetta Savio was to be of great help to him. With the liveliness of personal memories which could actually bring a tone of voice, a movement, a gesture back to life, she was to contribute to 'giving him back' the uncle who occupied more and more space in his life but whom he had only seen once, at Castelnuovo, at the age of six. And he was barely nine when his uncle died in 1860.

Schooling with Don Bosco

After kindergarten, he was sent to elementary school in Castelnuovo. Having attended five grades, always with good results, and been confirmed on 17 October 1860 (we do not know the date of his First Communion), in the summer of 1862, that phase of his schooling now being over, came the moment for making decisions.

To be truthful, his was not the classic situation of the very poor boy sent away to school after cliff-hanging uncertainties, with a host of illiterate brothers and relations. In that same year of 1862 his brother Natale had already completed first year junior high school in Turin, at Don Bosco's college in Valdocco. It would have been nothing out of the ordinary if Joseph had followed him. The obstacle, it seems, was a reluctance on his part of emotional origin, which he, many years later, described to his Missionary Sisters: 'There was my beloved mother who was sick by then, and I stayed at home and, I don't know, I suppose I was rather her pet. . . One of my elder brothers kept saying to me, "Why don't you come to college with me?" I would have gone but I felt bad about leaving mother. . . One day a priest came to our house with the local mayor; they had come to see my mother. When they saw me there, they said, "What's this boy doing? You ought to send him away to school." My mother replied, "I let him do as he pleases." When questioned, I did not know how to answer and began to cry. After that conversation, it was decided I should start my studies. You see, on the strength of what that fine mayor said, I made up my mind. Otherwise I should have stayed at home. . .'

As a matter of fact, Marianna Cafasso had already made a few plans for her sons, with the advice of her brother Fr Giuseppe while he was still alive (he died on 23 June 1860), and of her brother-in-law Fr Giovanni Allamano, the fatherless children's guardian. The two priests certainly planned on sending one or other of their nephews to the seminary and it seems Fr Cafasso actually had Joseph in mind. He had too been somewhat uncertain as to the suitability of sending him to study with Don Bosco, judging his institutes still not to be sufficiently selective or sufficiently well organized. Nonetheless, that was where his mother first sent his brother Natale, then him, and later still the youngest of her sons, Ottavio.

So, accompanied by his uncle Fr Giovanni, Joseph Allamano entered Valdocco at the age of eleven, in the autumn of 1862. Turin at that moment was the restless new capital of the Kingdom of Italy, with its political and military worlds still in turmoil over Garibaldi's exploit that had ended bloodily on Aspromonte; the government of Urbano Rattazzi, under attack from all parties, finally collapsed in December, giving place to that of Luigi Carlo Farini. At Valdocco these were significant days too. The Salesian Society had already begun to consolidate, with twenty-two companions making their vows. The founder had confided a plan of his to some of the boys: the building of a 'grandiose' church which was to be the heart of the entire Salesian world and dedicated to Our Lady, Help of Christians. He had a place in mind for it too: a piece of land which had already been his but which he had been obliged to sell in 1854 and was now on the point of buying back.

At Valdocco, Joseph Allamano completed the entire five-year syllabus in four years only; on the advice of the superiors, he had skipped the fourth year, moving directly from third to fifth. And he was always among the first in class. After coming fifth in his first year, he came first in the next and second in the third. And in the final exams of the fifth year he came second as well.

Furthermore and above all, these years were a period of close and constant contact with Don Bosco, his 'regular confessor', as he was later to say. And if Don Bosco was away, he did not seek out anybody else: 'I confessed to him throughout the four years of my stay at the Oratory and, even though he was the superior, I always trusted him completely. . . It seemed to me, as his penitent, that he could read my heart and foresee many things about me.' These are fragments from his testimony at the process for Don Bosco's beatification. On another occasion, while talking to the missionaries, he recalled his severity too: 'I remember having been severely rebuked for reading Guerrazzi's novel *Beatrice Cenci* during the holidays, and this rebuke made a great impression on me and stood me in good stead for the future.'

Don Bosco for his part probably saw this lad from his own home town as already following in Giovanni Cagliero's footsteps: student, priest, Salesian priest. However, with junior high school behind him, on Sunday 19 August 1866, Joseph Allamano left Valdocco for the customary holidays with his mind made up that he would not be going back there any more. He had not said goodbye to anyone, least of all Don Bosco, wanting to spare him the pain of what was a kind of desertion, and possibly fearing he might not know how to resist if Don Bosco were to invite him to stay. He knew his powers of persuasion all too well. No one found it easy to say no to Don Bosco.

15

Had he at this point already firmly made up his mind to become a priest, by choosing the diocesan way of the seminary? It is hard to say; the inward maturing of such decisions cannot be subjected to the calendar, to a precise dating. The fact remains that Joseph Allamano went home to his family at the age of fifteen, in the summer of the Third War of Independence — the one which after ill-starred battles by land and sea was however to acquire the Veneto for a future united Italy. He went home and within a few weeks had informed everyone, if not of an accomplished and irrevocable fact, then at least of a decision he had made and was now about to put into effect. On a Sunday in October, he received the cassock from the parish priest, Michele Antonio Cinzano, in the parish church of Castelnuovo. He had made his choice calmly and finally, even overcoming his brothers' bewilderment and prudential suggestions: 'If you were to leave the seminary after a year or two, you wouldn't have a penny to your name...' Wouldn't it be wiser to take more thought over a decision of this sort and meanwhile attend a state high school in any case? No, the necessary thought has already been taken, there will be no further change of mind. 'The Lord is calling me *today*.'

On the first Sunday in November 1866, the city of Turin, which had reluctantly ceded the role of capital to Florence, received a small consolation prize. King Victor Emmanuel decided that here, in the old capital, a very solemn ceremony should take place: the reception of the delegates bringing the results of the plebiscite held in the Veneto provinces over their union with Italy. 'Today,' said the King, 'is the finest day of my life.' And so, more or less, said the fifteen-year-old country lad from Monferrato after his clothing. His biographer Lorenzo Sales notes: 'I have heard him say it was one of the finest days of his life.'

Seminarian in Turin

Accompanied by his uncle from Passerano, Joseph Allamano entered the Metropolitan Seminary in Turin on 1 November 1866. And no doubt he noted the strong contrast there was between the turmoil (and the architecture

16

too) at Valdocco and the majestic elegance of the structures designed and carried out by Juvara in honour of the Catholic priesthood. And how the gravity of the masters, beginning with the rector, Canon Alessandro Vogliotti, and the spiritual director, Fr Giuseppe Soldati, accorded with the surroundings. All this made the happiest of first impressions on the budding seminarian. And with the passing of time he was also to discover a harmony between the institution's rules and his own inclinations. Yes, inside here there was an order, a regularity, an 'exactness' as they used to say at home, which was always to please him. He even liked those fussy arrangements intended to foresee and legislate for every eventuality, which drove many of his fellow-students to the point of desperation. There was no minute in anyone's day that might be called free, private, disposable as the seminarian might judge best, even in those activities and occupations of the most lawful and laudable kind. In order to make all these boys into good priests and in order to give the faithful the best pastors, it was thought absolutely essential that there should be total planning of every hour and every minute of this segregated life, where contacts with the outside world (in which the new priests would be called to act) were considered to be harmful, as also the vehicles of information about that world: newspapers. Even the Catholic press at times was little more than tolerated.

As regards Turin and its seminary, we should perhaps add something that, to the compilers of the regulations, may have seemed one further incentive for the argus-eyed control of its future priests. The Metropolitan Seminary of Turin had been re-opened after fourteen years of closure. Archbishop Luigi Fransoni had decided to bolt its door in 1848 after the clerics had appeared in the cathedral for Pontifical High Mass on Christmas Day 1847 sporting the tricolor cockade on their liturgical vestments; and after, in Juvara's court-yard — February 1848, with Turin in the seventh heaven over the promised Statute and the war with Austria — these same seminarians had held a demonstration to the singing of the revolutionary anthem: '*I figli d'Italia son tutti Balilla*'. (Italy's sons are all Balilla, young fascist soldiers).

This closure of the seminary was a fine present for the Archbishop to make to the government, for it immediately

17

used the building for its military requirements (hospital, magazine, barracks). Only in 1862 after Archbishop Fransoni's death in exile did the seminary revert to curial ownership. And only from December 1863 was it able to resume academic activity.

Perhaps this past had an influence on the drafting and application of the new regulations, it being believed that the events of 1847–1848 were exclusively due to a culpable relaxation of discipline.

At that point in time when Joseph Allamano began his studies at the seminary, the diocese of Turin was still without a bishop. For the previous sixteen years it had been governed by a vicar-general, who at that moment was Mgr Giuseppe Zappata. It was under his authority that the rules for the life of the new seminary had been drawn up; and, like it or not, the seminary was saddled with them for good. The youthful Allamano assured himself that every article, prescription, obligation, prohibition contributed to the unique purpose of making him into a worthy priest. And so he accepted them all. As Fr Sales relates, he took pains to learn all these rules by heart 'so as not to break any one of them', not even those that little accorded with his own not particularly robust health. When he had been placed with Don Bosco, his uncle-priest of Passerano paid extra for about two months for him to have white coffee in the morning. Here in the seminary, by contrast, no extras of any sort. Breakfast, according to the rules, consisted of a small loaf of bread which those in charge placed on each bed at daybreak.

2

'Massive ignorance'

'In my youth, my health was much more delicate than it is now: once a fortnight I had a migraine which would bring me to a standstill. I would go into the refectory and eat a few scraps so that no one noticed what was going on; in class, I would sit holding my forehead in my hands as if I was studying, and so no one ever noticed that there was something wrong with me.' This was how in maturity Joseph Allamano recalled his fluctuating health in the seminary.

Hardly agreeable fluctuations, since he had a rather frail physique, not really suited to the strain of study and the rigour of the timetables. Already during his first year he was forced to spend a month in bed and undergo a series of cuppings, which then caused a haemorrhage. And his disposition to migraine began precisely with that. (To anticipate: at the army medicals in Asti in February 1872, he was to be 'exempted', that is to say, rejected for military service, having — the Medical Corps Captain noted — 'a very healthy physique but being of delicate constitution and exhausted by studying'.)

He was exactly like that. He overdid things. At the outset he had intended to add the subjects taught at state secondary school to those he was studying in the seminary. Was this perhaps a precaution in case he were to leave, according to the pessimistic hypothesis put forward by his brothers? We do not know. It may even have been an effort to be better informed before being ordained; for the sake of the priesthood therefore. One of his deepest convictions was: 'Perhaps an ignorant priest does more harm than a wicked one', with another: 'St Francis de Sales wrote that what caused Protestantism was the ignorance of the clergy of those days.' And among his notes on a course of spiritual exercises we find a preacher's exhortation noted

19

down: 'Second to a reputation for dissolute living, for a priest a reputation for being ignorant is the most shameful and damaging to his ministry.'

Year by year his results remained very good in all subjects, principally because he was an untiring swot. What is more, he was very systematic and efficient as regards notes, summaries, orderly abridgements of reading matter and courses; those pages were still to be of service to him even in old age. He put as much order into the planning of his interior life. Superiors and the spirit of the age encouraged the keeping of spiritual diaries, journals of the soul, regulations for private devotion and for studies. And so he too did this (and was to go on doing so all his life), opting for the concrete regulation of timetables, duties and private reading.

These regulations served him too for his self-analysis, for tracking down errors and weaknesses, for organizing self-correction down to the minutest particulars. He had special problems with pride, 'my predominant fault', and to combat this he imposed reflections and special prayers on himself, and careful attention to the maxims of the saints. (Something of the same sort seems to have been going on some thirty years later in Bergamo with the seminarian Angelo Giuseppe Roncalli [the future Pope John XXIII]; he too being quick to accuse himself of this capital sin in *The Journal of a Soul*: '. . . I am so interlarded with pride that I fall again, even unawares, when I think I am doing well and being charitable. . . This very day, for instance, I carried the thurible for the first time at Solemn Vespers and I cut the figure I deserved, I who am always picking holes in the others. Everybody laughed behind my back, and it serves me right'.)

It happened from time to time that he helped fellow-students in crisis, with a remarkable authoritativeness which he was acquiring, whether as a result of his studies or from that courteous firmness of character of which he already gave evidence and which made his replies and exhortations so persuasive. Many years later he was to say: 'When I left the seminary, I was calm. I knew what I had to do.' From the recollections and testimony of various fellow-students, one is given to understand that he appeared exactly so, prepared and sure, even before completing his studies.

Two years of philosophy, five of theology: grades always very good. A tranquil progress towards the priesthood, without halting, without rushing. Joseph Allamano was to finish his course as a seminarian at the same pace as on his first day. He did however have to make some sacrifices: for instance his dream of becoming a missionary. With his uncertain health it was out of the question (as it had also been for Don Bosco). At the time there was nothing vague for him about the missionary ideal: it had the physical dimensions and the face of Guglielmo Massaia, the great *Abuna* of the Ethiopians, whom he had seen arriving one day in the courtyard at Valdocco amid wild rejoicing.

And besides, he had begun to make a discovery. He had re-encountered Giuseppe Cafasso: no longer the priest his uncle, the familiar figure of Castelnuovo, but the Cafasso of Turin, of the cathedral and the confessional, the master. Step by step, he identified his footprints on his own path of future priest in the memory of other priests; he heard his uncle's voice speaking through his own teachers. Even during his days at Valdocco, he would often visit his tomb in the Turin cemetery. But now he was rediscovering him alive, ever more present. It was almost inevitable that he should think of writing his life and that he should begin the work of collecting material for a biography.

Joseph Allamano's tranquil progress was however inter-rupted by rude blows raining down on his family. In 1868 in the month of May (dedicated to Our Lady), his brother Ottavio was ringing the bells of the parish church for the evening Angelus when his left arm got tangled up in the rope, which fractured it and stretched it cruelly too. First aid given on the spot made matters worse and when finally a compe-tent doctor arrived from Turin, there was no appealing his judgement: amputation as soon as possible. For Joseph, this was a special grief since he had always looked on Ottavio as his younger brother, the one who had been his school-fellow at Valdocco. Fr Giovanni the priest-uncle then came to Ottavio's rescue and the latter later graduated in law at the University of Turin.

Marianna Cafasso was already beginning to suffer from pains in the spine in 1866 before Joseph Allamano entered the seminary, as we have seen; and this was one of the reasons why her son was sad to be parted from her. But his mother was quick to remove that particular obstacle: 'I let him do as he likes.' Her illness grew more and more serious until she became an invalid confined to her bed. But that was not the end of it. In bed she went blind and later lost her hearing too. As long as she could hear, during his holidays from the seminary, Joseph would read to her, talk to her, spending all the time he had free from church services with her. When she became deaf, he used to communicate with her by code, giving her loving little pats on the hand, so that they could understand each other. And at times his mother would have to send him out of the room: 'Go and get some fresh air. . .'

Close to one another as they were, Joseph could not be present to assist her in her last moments. Quite unknown to him, she died on 15 December 1869. One of those ghastly accidents had happened, according to the testimony of Sr Maria degli Angeli Vassallo of Castelnuovo, a Consolata Missionary Sister: 'Fr Allamano told us that when she died he was not present, being at the seminary, and that the person who was supposed to bring him the message had forgotten the letter in his pocket.' In Fr Sales' biography it says that he was neither able to see her when she was dead nor could he attend her funeral. He knew however that in her last moments she was certain he was beside her because someone there kept patting her hand just as he would.

He was then forced to go home after Christmas in a state of general depression aggravated by bleeding from the mouth. He had been granted a fortnight's leave but had to stay in Castelnuovo for two months. On returning, he resumed his studies. The exams for third year theology went as well for him as the others.

Meanwhile, after seventeen years, Turin once again had an archbishop, though only for a little while. Bishop Alessandro Riccardi of Netro took possession of the diocese in 1867; though already sick, he attended the First Vatican Council, but his failing health forced him to leave Rome even before the Franco-Prussian War and the entry of Italian troops into the city suspended the Council. He died in December 1870. Nomination of his successor was one of those affairs which in those days took place in more or less clandestine conversations between emissaries of the government and emissaries of the Pope, given that at the time Holy See and State of Italy officially ignored each other's existence.

The problem lay in this: the Pope naturally intended to give every diocese its own bishop but refused officially to inform the government of those named, since to do so would have entailed recognizing Victor Emmanuel II as king of Italy. And the government, lacking this recognition, refused the *exequatur* (or the go-ahead) to those named, so that they could not enter into possession of their dioceses. A compromise formula was then found: where the name of a new bishop was found acceptable to the Holy See and the government, the civil power allowed him to be installed, being satisfied with mere notification; but it did not concede him the so-called temporalities. That is to say, it did not allow him to touch the material assets of the diocese, and these remained frozen. Consequently many newly appointed bishops were unable to occupy their episcopal palaces. And this was the case in Turin, where in 1871 the seminary lodged Archbishop Riccardi's successor, Archbishop Lorenzo Gastaldi, aged fifty-six, Turin-born of a family of Chierese stock. A great friend of Don Bosco's and his collaborator for some time already (he even remembered him in his will), he had actually been suggested to Pius IX by Don Bosco in 1867 as Bishop of Saluzzo and three years later as Archbishop of Turin. To the founder of the Salesians, the Pope had even let slip his intention of doing 'something more' for Gastaldi, in recognition of his zeal during the Council for the definition of papal infallibility. The 'more' was in all likelihood being created Cardinal. And Don Bosco in turn let slip what the Pope had said, to Gastaldi — not noticing that the latter found this sort of protectorate extremely irksome.

Under Archbishop Gastaldi, Joseph Allamano went

through the various canonical stages towards the priesthood. On 25 May 1872, with the minor orders, he received the tonsure making him a member of the Turinese clergy: 'incardinated' into the diocese, as the phrase is. And for this he had had to provide himself with the so-called ecclesiastical patrimony: that is to say, be the owner of sufficient resources at least to guarantee his survival. As stated in the episcopal ordinances, a capital sum was required that *'referat bis centum et quadraginta libellas italicas'*, that is to say, bringing in not less than 240 lire a year. His own patrimony consisted of inherited property.

On 21 December 1872, he received the subdiaconate after making his retreat at Chieri. This was a most important, indeed decisive step, since the subdeacon also made the vow of perpetual chastity. Preparation for and performance of the rite were therefore both orientated, as the climate of the age required, towards consideration of the tremendous commitment that each young man was making, and of the risk of damnation hanging over anyone who might violate the commitments entered into at this moment. To Joseph Allamano and his companions, Archbishop Gastaldi said in solemn tones: 'Today, Subdeacons, a crown has been placed upon your head which will remain there for eternity: either to your glory in heaven or to your torment in hell. So act, that I shall never have to repent of ordaining you and that you will never live to curse this hour.'

On 23 March 1873, he received the diaconate, and as deacon he gave his first sermon in the church at Castelnuovo on the feast of the Assumption.

The summer of 1873 witnessed in Turin a unique splendid occasion: the visit of the Shah of Persia, 'blazing with diamonds', whereas the King of Denmark behaved much more modestly, arriving *incognito* and calling himself the Count of Falster. But Turin was to see other things too that year. The great church of Our Lady, Help of Christians, the heart of the Salesian Society, had been consecrated on 9 June 1868. The following year, the Society received papal approval under that name. In 1872 the Congregation of the Daughters of Our Lady, Help of Christians, was formed, with the first ten girls assembling to take the veil with Maria Mazzarello (for this duty, as we have already said, Don

24

Bosco had originally had the school mistress Benedetta Savio in mind). On St Joseph's Day, 1873, in the chapel of the Young Artisans' Centre, a small group of priests and seminarians gathered for what was virtually a clandestine ceremony: before Leonardo Murialdo and in the presence of two witnesses, three priests and two seminarians made their vows. And with this act the Pious Congregation of St Joseph for the Instruction of the Young — the Josephites — came into being.

At about the same time, the story of 'the procession of saints' was doing the rounds of Turin. As recorded by Jose Cottino in his biography of Luigi Anglesio, Giuseppe Cottolengo's successor: 'A group of English tourists visiting Turin were directed to the Cottolengo Hospital. "A marvellous charitable work," they were told, "and besides you will find a saint there." They went, and at the end of the visit they asked Fr Anglesio himself if they could have a word with the saint whom they had heard about. The priest replied, "If you want to see a saint, you must go to Borgo San Donato, to the Academy of St Zita." At St Zita lived the Venerable Francis Faà di Bruno, animator in social work among domestic servants, who also spoke English. Faà di Bruno received them politely, showed them round the institution and, at the same request, smilingly sent them on to Valdocco to see Don Bosco. Don Bosco merely repeated the whole process by sending them back again to the Cottolengo.'

Ordained priest

In the seminary meanwhile, for the academic year 1872–1873, he was 'Chapel Prefect' with and over two other students who were 'dormitory prefects'. In a word, says Fr Sales, he had officially become 'head student of his year and had to supervise, keep in order and admonish the rest.' And this was a sort of official seal on the good-natured authority he already exercised by his native qualities among his fellow-students.

The time arrived for ordinations, but for him this meant

a further period of waiting. He had not yet reached the age of twenty-two and a half at the date for the June ordinations so, owing to this 'defect of age', he was compelled to wait until September. The retreat, assiduous attention to the preaching of this or that preacher (this was to be one of his life-long interests) and holidays at Castelnuovo filled his time while awaiting the great day. He wrote to a friend whom he had known at Don Bosco's Oratory and who too was to be ordained in 1873, Pietro Cantarella, who later became a parish priest in the Diocese of Alessandria: 'How can I make sure I am properly disposed, now that holy ordination to the priesthood is so near — the object of so much yearning, the aim of so many years of study?' The letter is dated 31 August 1873; ordination was twenty days away and the young man was naturally tensed towards the event, entirely concentrated on it: 'The holidays have never seemed so long to me and I should like to hide away from every human eye, so as only to think about the solemn act awaiting me; instead I am forced to get involved in all sorts of distracting matters. . .' He is conscious of the enormous value of the priestly state, yet does not seem overawed by it, as it happens to some people and as certain sermons tend to encourage. He seems rather fascinated by it. He speaks of 'awe, ever growing the further I advance, of that sublimest dignity with which I am about to be clothed.' But immediately he then expresses his 'great trust in God who himself wills to work these marvels in me that he has worked in many another soul.'

And on Saturday 20 September he is there in the cathedral with two other deacons, Francesco Ghione and Vincenzo Roppolo, before Archbishop Lorenzo Gastaldi. First, the preliminary questions and answers, then the insistent prayers the Church utters at these solemn moments, and now at last the laying on of hands, making him a priest forever. Then the bishop addresses all three: 'My dear sons, take serious thought over what you have now done. You have dedicated yourselves entirely to God, to work and to suffer for his glory and for the salvation of your neighbour. Great sacrifices await you, but with God's guarantee you will overcome them. And what consolations await you too! . . . Take heart therefore, be generous with the Lord; now only give

26

pride of place to hard work; do not assume this is the time for rest; rest will be ours in heaven. . .'

In the month of November, after the holidays, Fr Joseph Allamano entered the Pastoral Institute in Turin to complete his training. Since 1871 the Pastoral Institute had been at the Shrine of the Consolata; the director was Canon Bartolomeo Roetti; Mgr Giovanni Battista Bertagna of Castelnuovo d'Asti held the chair of Moral Theology. The young priest had barely become acquainted with his surroundings when a new proposal arrived: that he should go back to the seminary with the post of first assistant, or prefect. In other words, the job of supervising the theology students individually, in their studies and in their other activities, intervening too to correct mistakes and negligences. The Archbishop explained to him that he was to let nothing pass, not even the most trivial shortcomings: 'Like a music teacher, who will not let a wrong note pass, even if it is only a little one. . .'

And as for Fr Joseph, what did he think about this work and how it should be done? Years later, while writing to the theology student Luigi Boccardo, summoned to the same task, he was to explain: 'You see, among seminary prefects, some manage to do real harm; many, indeed most, are useless creatures, even if they cannot actually be called harmful on account of their uselessness; very few discharge that office well.' And to discharge it well, he goes on, you must first respect the rules, supervise and intervene straightforwardly and often 'correct with some indication of punishment . . . for this or that shortcoming.' Furthermore it is better to deal with trifling matters in private without always making a song and dance, so that students realize the prefect is not 'a fault-finder anxious to get them into trouble with the superiors, but a friend who loves them and has their best interests at heart.' In this letter Fr Joseph gives an unintended portrait of himself, and not merely as a seminary prefect.

The new post did not however stop him from following the courses at the Pastoral Institute as a non-resident. And further, in 1874, he also managed to graduate with distinction at the Pontifical Faculty of Theology just instituted by Archbishop Gastaldi, the one previously existing in the Royal University having been suppressed.

But at this point these exertions took their toll. At the end of the academic year he again relapsed into exhaustion, made worse by a serious recurrence of haemoptysis. He got better slowly during the holidays and was fit enough in the autumn to resume his work in the seminary and his courses at the Pastoral Institute. In the exercise of his ministry, he had trained himself to celebrate Mass later and later in the morning, naturally with strict fasting from midnight in accordance with the rules of the time; thus, he thought, he would be prepared for celebrating the last Mass of the morning, always assigned to the junior curate. At this moment he saw the future in these terms. Indeed, he actually anticipated it a little during the summer holidays, for he spent them at Passerano, helping his uncle Fr Giovanni in his parish.

The time for a new appointment would probably be the end of the academic year 1874–1875, or at the latest the beginning of the next: at the expiry, in a word, of a two-year stint in the seminary. An exception was made in his case however: in the autumn of 1875 he was confirmed in his post for a further year.

Fr Giovanni of Passerano

Then he received another, and certainly unexpected, assignment. Fr Luigi Anglesio, Fr Cottolengo's successor in running the Little House of Divine Providence, asked him to become confessor to the Taidine Sisters. This was in 1876, according to Fr Sales: Fr Joseph was twenty-five and the Taidines were a very special family among those brought into existence by Fr Cottolengo. It all began with a rescue home, where he intended to take in women who wanted to escape from a life on the streets. From this group, housed in Gassino Torinese, a few expressed a desire to form themselves into a religious community. Fr Cottolengo encouraged the scheme by giving them a rule of life based on that of the Carmelites and by calling in several Carmelite nuns to guide the new community. The name 'Taidine' is derived from St Thais, the altogether legendary figure of a courtesan who repented to lead a deeply religious life. Fr

Allamano replied to this suggestion by urging his own inexperience: he was still too young, having barely started hearing confessions. But Fr Anglesio had a short and conclusive answer: 'Fr Cafasso too began with young ladies.' There was nothing for it but to accept, and so Fr Joseph did, devoting himself to this task to the utmost of his abilities.

Well: Fr Anglesio, Fr Cottolengo, Fr Cafasso. A little group of saints, one might say, begins to be concerned with him. Without yet realizing, Joseph Allamano is being drawn into their orbit.

At last the summer holidays of 1876 arrived, after one of the longest and coldest winters Turin had ever known. (Seventy centimetres of snow fell at a time; on some days the city was a white wilderness.) Joseph Allamano left for the country, Passerano. But this was to be the last time: his uncle Fr Giovanni, not in fact particularly old, being sixty-eight, was dying. His nephew assisted and comforted him to the end, with other priests. But of these there was one who did not know how to deal with the dying, and bothered Fr Giovanni by suggesting invocations and prayers without respite, until he summoned the breath to say to his nephew: 'For heaven's sake, get rid of this tiresome fellow!'

On 21 August, Fr Giovanni breathed his last after thirty-five years as parish priest, and his nephew temporarily substituted for him as acting vicar, with his usual 'exactness'. Even though the job was provisional, he was not the one to improvise. There was the usual diligent preparation for each ministerial act, each sermon had its scheme of points, and for each he wrote out the complete text, in Piedmontese.

The parishioners would have been glad to have him as his uncle's successor, and he would have liked it too. The leading family, that of the Counts Radicati, even took steps to this end, but in Turin other plans were being made for Fr Joseph. And on his return to the seminary in the early days of November, he found that his appointment as assistant had not been renewed after all and that the Archbishop was waiting for him. Without beating about the bush, the Archbishop informed him of his new appointment: spiritual director at the Turin seminary.

On the responsibilities of this office Archbishop Gastaldi

gave very wide terms of reference, which Fr Igino Tubaldo summarises as follows: 'He was very zealously to attend to whatever might serve to form the students' spirit in accordance with the rules laid down by Jesus Christ and the Church for his ministers. . . to accustom them to judge everything by the light of faith, to maintain union with God and to be filled with the spirit of prayer; he was, with great constancy, prudence and charity, to study the temperament and attitudes of mind and heart of each student; to seek out their virtues and defects, so as to be able to judge whether they were suitable or not for the priestly ministry; to admonish them over their faults, always employing great charity; to show that he had confidence in them and always to behave as a friend and father to them. . .' And as if this were not enough, he was also to supervise every moment and action of every seminarian, while living continually among them.

To see how many matters a spiritual director is meant to deal with, over and above those already mentioned, it is enough to read some of the 'Notices' which Joseph Allamano had to bring to the attention of the students and which were of course 'exactly' expressed. First of all, they were to pay attention during sermons, share with faith in the prayers in chapel and at Mass, and not make a noise by sneezing or blowing their noses. And then: 'When feeding the cat, do not soil the floor.' 'It is forbidden to write out music in the study-room.' 'No talking or writing in the lavatories.' 'No singing or whistling.'

It was an enormous responsibility: it consisted in assessing each individual's suitability for the priesthood and thus contributing to his being accepted or rejected. It required rare perspicacity, much attention, much watchfulness too. It was easy to get oneself hated by these lads. But the ones over whom Allamano kept watch finished up by loving him, as numerous testimonies show. He conquered them with his delicacy of touch and his pleasant manner with all. Many speak of his gentleness, which however was never attended with any flexibility over the rules or any relaxation of discipline. On the contrary: his sweetness of manner was one of the weapons for getting himself obeyed.

So the Archbishop commanded and Fr Joseph accepted.

He would be a spiritual director. And scarcely was he appointed, than he was one. He served no apprenticeship, as Fr Sales so effectively explains: 'Some people thought the new director, at least for the first few days, would appear perturbed, or have difficulty in coming to terms with this very important job, or be profuse in apologetic little speeches, protests of inability and other formalities of the kind. Nothing of the sort. He took up the job that same day and on that same day began performing his duties with such calmness and command of his actions as if he had never done anything else. The clerics were amazed.'

3

Check to the Jansenists

At Joseph Allamano's debut in his new job, he suffered a new attack of haemoptysis, which struck him in the second half of November 1876. It was more severe than the previous ones, so much so that he was given the last rites. His recovery however was pretty quick and he resumed his studies: he was preparing for the competitive examinations for being accepted, 'admitted', to the teaching staff of the Theological Faculty. On 22 December he passed the first exam, known as private, thus finding himself sent on to the second, in the presence of the entire teaching staff and the Archbishop too. This was on 12 June 1877. Examiners and candidate conversed in Latin and in the end the solemn announcement *'probatus est'* ('he has passed the exams') sanctioned his acceptance into the teaching body.

For the spiritual director of a seminary, the qualification of 'collegiate doctor' confers considerable prestige. But his influence in that institution primarily depends on what kind of man he is. The students were not slow to grasp that this director would not make reductions in, nor would he concede any departure from, the rules, however trifling they might be. In this field he was certainly no innovator. He did however know how spontaneously to identify with them, provided it was a question of helping them to obey. He did not cut himself off from the superiors nor did he play the officer in command. Yet every student knew that he could confidently turn to him, especially in moments of crisis; each of them knew himself to be thoroughly known by him. Even too much so, on occasion; he seemed to be able to read their minds. One of them says: 'We all saw to it that we did not entertain idle thoughts, thinking that we should be found out by the director.' And his subdued method of rebuke too left its mark. Another of his pupils: 'I am not afraid of the rector's rages, they pass like a summer storm. . . but that "I'm sorry, I'm sorry", said by the director in that quiet voice, goes to my heart and leaves me in confusion for at least three months.'

Rules and prohibitions however could not effectively prevent people inside the seminary from talking or whispering about the latest events, for in the diocesan sphere there were real bombshells. In September 1876, Archbishop Gastaldi brusquely relieved Mgr Bertagna of his duties as professor of Moral Theology at the Pastoral Institute. This action had dramatic repercussions, given Mgr Bertagna's prestige for learning and for integrity of life (a bit less for character). But it was not unexpected. The Archbishop had previously sent him certain suggestions clearly put, which had the flavour of rebuke about them. In 1875, he had had recourse to a kind of referendum among the hundreds of diocesan priests, asking each for a written opinion on the moral theology being taught at the Pastoral Institute. Apparently a large majority had given unfavourable assessments, even though a number had taken up very definite positions in favour. Finally, before the academic year 1876–1877 began, Mgr Bertagna was informed of this humiliating measure. (Which he nonetheless received with great dignity. He then accepted an invitation from the Bishop of Asti, who summoned him to his diocese and made him his vicar general.)

The Bertagna affair was one more residual 'passage of arms' in a conflict that had been troubling the Piedmontese Church for decades. As long as it existed, the Theological Faculty of the Royal University had been the stronghold of those who trained new priests in an austere and demanding moral system, as the indispensable medicine against the faith ill-lived and a debased morality. For them, God was above all Justice, and anyone who was not prepared to acknowledge this for fear of alarming the faithful was in reality deceiving them and helping them along the road to ruin. And to these apostles of rigour, their opponents gave the name 'Jansenist'.

In opposition to the University stood the Pastoral Institute, from its very beginning the bastion of Alphonsian moral theology: that is to say, the system taught in the eighteenth century by Alphonsus de'Liguori, beatified by Pius

VII in 1816 and canonized by Gregory XVI in 1839. Combatted as 'benignists' or laxists by the champions of rigorism, the followers of Alphonsus certainly did not intend to tolerate immorality. They tried, rather, by emphasizing the Almighty's mercy, to encourage the sinner by offering him a salvation that was ever-attainable and by allowing him a little bit of credit. That is to say, by absolving anyone in confession who gave signs of genuine repentance, even if knowing he was likely to relapse. In such a case, by contrast, the rigorist party insisted on the duty of postponing absolution and in certain cases actually of refusing it.

Fr Cafasso's teaching at the Pastoral Institute, entirely orientated on the Alphonsian doctrine (enriched by his own acumen and commonsense) had been constantly praised in his lifetime and after his death. Suffice it to recall what Don Bosco said about him: 'Some call him a new St Louis Gonzaga for his innocence and purity of manners; others call him a St Francis de Sales for kindness, patience and charity; some call him a Vincent de Paul for the great charity with which he treats every kind of unfortunate. And there are those who do not hesitate to call him a St Charles Borromeo for the harshness of his way of life and the austerity with which he treats himself. And while they marvel at the harshness of his life-style, they call him a new St Alphonsus for sweetness, patience and charity.'

And Bertagna's authority had consistently increased just because he continued in the Cafassian line. And also because he went on in his own way too: certainly a preacher of compassion and kindness, but also a person somewhat prickly in his integrity.

He had enemies in the diocese: certain elderly priests, trained at the University, who regarded all the junior clergy coming into the parishes from the Pastoral Institute as laxist. And he found himself on collision course with the Archbishop and the latter's wide, extremely wide, concept of episcopal authority. Hence, to start with, the more or less open disagreement and finally his dismissal. With which, Fr Sales observes, Archbishop Gastaldi was able to calm down the rigorists outside the Pastoral Institute but had put an end to tranquillity within it. Indeed, the new professor, Canon Ludovico Chicco, instantly found the whole student body against him. After a painful exchange of accusations, excuses and new accusations, Canon Chicco resigned from the post in November 1879. The Archbishop then closed the Pastoral Institute down and transferred the students from the Consolata to the seminary; and he decided to supervise the teaching of moral theology in person.

Very tough years for Archbishop Lorenzo Gastaldi. In January 1878, King Victor Emmanuel II having died in Rome, he had been among those bishops who had most hotly and publicly taken part in the Italian struggle. And had thus offered — as though there were need of more — fresh arguments to his opponents who, by means of articles in the secular press and anonymous libels, united in calling on him to resign. For them, everything about the Archbishop was suspect: first, he came from the Royal University with its rigorist and 'Jansenist' Faculty; after which he had forthwith entered Antonio Rosmini's Institute of Charity (actually spending about ten years in Great Britain as a missionary); and hence it was impossible for him not to have retained a touch of that Rosminianism which was so unpopular in the highest reaches of the Church, especially so with the new Pope, Leo XIII. And then, wasn't his severity to the Pastoral Institute one further phase in his anti-Alphonsian vendetta? In all, wasn't this Gastaldi more than a little tainted with Liberalism, like so many of those damned rigorists?

But this was not all; there was more to come. The secular press went on attacking him as the champion of authoritarianism and enemy of liberty. And when this had reached its most acute and unendurable phase, to top it all came his quarrel with Don Bosco. The latter was partly to blame. The concessions made by Pope Pius IX to the founder of the Salesians in order to encourage his work, often ended up infringing on the diocesan bishop's authority and responsibility in the capital matter of ordaining new priests. Archbishop Gastaldi frequently found Don Bosco going above his head, determined to get everything done on the instant, to have more priests as fast as possible; and Rome too for its part seemed to encourage these methods, just as if bishops did not matter. And as if he, Archbishop Gastaldi, in particular did not matter, although at the

Vatican Council in 1870 he had been such a champion of papal supremacy.

The quarrel was becoming so acute that Leo XIII was compelled to exert his authority and impose 'truce' on the contending parties.

Bad times. But this was not the entire picture in Turin. In those same years and days, in the city and diocese, there were circulating at least a score of persons, today already raised to the altars or near to being so: saints, blessed, servants of God. All at work, doing different jobs with different ups and downs, within this same perturbed Church of Turin; all of them in varying relationship with Archbishop Gastaldi; and more than one in conflict with him at any given moment. From this arose the tendency to regard him as the opponent of the saints, someone who was always in the wrong and who made a mess of everything. And this would have been the worst injustice to him.

As his most recent biographer, G. Tuninetti, says: 'The conflict between Don Bosco and Gastaldi was also, objectively speaking, the conflict between the Archbishop of Turin and the Holy See, between the exercise of episcopal authority and that of papal supremacy. And this on the morrow of Vatican I which had defined papal supremacy and infallibility. Gastaldi's behaviour in this context above all, but also in others, can be seen too as symptomatic of ecclesiological unease at a dominant ecclesiology tending cavalierly to override episcopal authority.'

The saints who had clashed with him were no less saintly because of this. And he, we may perhaps say, refused ever to be any the less bishop. A refusal sometimes expressed in less than timely terms; yet, as regards the substance, hard to turn into matter for indictment.

'Go to the Consolata'

From his advanced observation post in the seminary, Fr Allamano naturally saw everything day by day, and who knows how much he may have heard? Anyhow, when the Archbishop suspended the activities of the Pastoral Institute, it was to Fr Allamano at the seminary that the priests from the Consolata were entrusted. A letter of his to his friend Fr Cantarella contains a fleeting reference to this and to the 'changes in things'. But we do not know anything else about his thoughts and state of mind in the midst of the cyclone. (Canon Roetti, dismissed from his rectorship of the Pastoral Institute and the Consolata, simply walked out leaving the keys with the bursar.)

The year 1880 began with a bereavement in the Allamano family. On 26 January, having barely set up house in Via Carlo Alberto, his younger brother Ottavio died of pneumonia at the age of twenty-six. In October 1877 he had married Benedettina Turco of Castelnuovo, by whom he had one daughter, Pia Clotilde. He had already taken his law degree in July 1878 and was at the start of a promising career. He died very quickly, assisted by Fr Joseph.

In September 1880 while with the clerics at the Turin Hermitage, a surprise! Summoned by the Archbishop, he was offered the appointment as rector of the Consolata, which also comprised the rectorship of the Pastoral Institute and of the Shrine of Sant' Ignazio at Lanzo torinese. The Archbishop had his answer ready to the predictable objection of the twenty-nine-year-old priest: all the better if he was young, since, if he made mistakes, he would have time to put them right. And the Archbishop pressed him, virtually pushed him, into taking up the post without delay.

On 2 October 1880, Joseph Allamano walked into the Shrine of the Consolata without warning and unannounced (the decree of appointment was only to be issued in November). Inside, it was like being a stowaway. There he was, at the apex of fifteen centuries of history, traditions and legends about the place where, long ago, between the fourth and fifth centuries St Maximus, the first bishop, had built a church in honour of St Andrew. And in it he had placed a picture of Mary and her Child, about which tales have later blossomed, hard to check, of lengthy disappearances and miraculous rediscoveries. The church nonetheless has a well-documented history: the people of Turin have gathered in this place of worship, century after century, to pray in times of suffering, wars, epidemics, public disasters — and in times of peace too. Generation after generation, they have made this church, dedicated to

Mary — first with the title of *Consolatrix* ('Consoler', or 'Comforter') and then of *Consolata* ('Consoled', or 'Comforted'), a popular expression that could be related to the biblical 'full of grace' — the church of the people of Turin. Gradually they have adopted it. And also, down the ages, they have moulded it into its present form and dimensions after a lengthy evolution, as described by Fr Igino Tubaldo:

'From the eleventh century until the days of Guarini (1679), the Church of Sant' Andrea, built by the monk Bruningo, consisted of three naves, differently orientated from the present structure. In the fifteenth century the building was lengthened. With this lengthening, a new facade was created, though without an entrance; the side entrance of Bruningo's church now became the main one. In the successive elaborations by Guarini (1679), Juvara (1714) and Ceppi in the days of Fr Allamano (1904), the original church was completely altered and took on that elliptical shape common to many Piedmontese churches of the seventeenth and eighteenth centuries (for example, the Vicoforte shrine at Mondovì and the parish church of Foglizzo). With Ceppi, the Shrine itself was enlarged with four oval chapels, to which access is given from the Church of Sant'Andrea by means of two flights of steps.'

Here various religious communities too succeeded one another. The Novalese Benedictines officiated for six hundred and seventy years, from 922 to 1589. They were followed by the Cistercians from 1589 to 1834; the Oblates of the Virgin Mary from 1834 until their expulsion in 1855. After that, the government installed the Friars Minor Observant. In 1871, the Pastoral Institute moved to the Consolata and a hospice for elderly priests was established there too. From 1871, the Turinese Curia took over the administration of the complex, naming one of its own priests as rector, while the Friars Minor continued to serve the Shrine under the rector's authority.

At the moment when Joseph Allamano began his rectorship, the situation was as follows: the Pastoral Institute was closed; the Friars Minor, advanced in years, were reduced to four. Besides the hospice for elderly priests, there was also a boarding house for young priests studying at the University. Old and young ate together. And there was no shortage of problems with those in poor health and dissatisfied with the way things were run.

Then he arrives with that courteous gravity, his dress always rigorously in order, his soft voice seeming to ask a favour even when giving an order. Perhaps he found the challenge rather tempting: every day to meet the whims of the poor old men, replying with his elegant brotherliness. Yes, some exercise of the virtue of charity was indicated. But all his dedication was not enough to keep this institution on its feet virtually without means, founded with such goodwill by Archbishop Allessandro Riccardi but so seriously underfunded. In the next couple of years the hospice was in fact to be closed down. Elsewhere in the diocese there was no lack of suitable places for retired priests.

The boarding house for the young priests would also cease to be, and then Rector Allamano would have to tackle the last problem of all. In a word, that of the Friars Minor, who were old, reduced to four and then to three. They were no longer in a state to look after the Shrine, but their dismissal had to take place with maximum dignity. To each of them Fr Allamano assigned a pension of 400 lire a year. And the Archbishop, when he came to hear of it, raised it to 500 from the diocesan funds.

These were only emergency measures, essential if the Shrine and what went with it were to survive. But still it was not the solution. Something quite different was needed. Above all what was needed was that the Pastoral Institute should resume functioning in all respects, and should function there, at the Consolata.

Joseph Allamano, as we have seen, arrived at his new post almost on tip-toe, on his own. But he stayed on his own for barely one day. Then he was joined by a priest even younger than himself: twenty-six. He was Giacomo Camisassa and in him Joseph Allamano met the most important and influential figure of his whole life.

Giacomo Camisassa was born in Caramagna Piemonte on 27 September 1854, the fifth of the six children of Gabriele and Agnese (born Perlo). After elementary school he became an apprentice blacksmith since the family's resources were minimal. He was doing well at his trade when his sister Anna Maria, the eldest of the family, in league with the parish priest, succeeded in making him resume his education: secondary school at Valdocco with Don Bosco,

39

where the boy also made his mark in the choir, thanks to his powerful voice. The choir master, Giovanni Cagliero, the future missionary and cardinal, was very enthusiastic about this, but the boy was keener on pursuing his studies — and in something else: he had decided to become a priest. A diocesan priest, however: another of Don Bosco's contributions to the Church of Turin. After junior years at Chieri, he attended the Metropolitan Seminary in Turin, where he got to know a spiritual director who made himself obeyed by everyone by giving subdued exhortations in a soft voice: Joseph Allamano. Ordained priest in July 1877, he graduated the following year, thrilling the whole theological faculty at the seminary. Then he attended the two-year course (the red-hot one) at the Pastoral Institute, after which, in the autumn of 1880, he was ready to go to Pecetto Torinese as junior curate.

But on his way he was stopped by a letter from Joseph Allamano who, before accepting Archbishop Gastaldi's invitation to run the Consolata, had made it a condition that he should be able to choose his own bursar. The Archbishop consented and Joseph named Camisassa. With those eyes that 'could read a man's thoughts', he had known him and sized him up in the seminary. And he wrote to him forthwith, inviting him to join him at the Consolata as soon as possible.

Allamano walked into the Shrine on 2 October 1880. Camisassa came on 3 October. For forty-two years they lived and laboured together. In his letter of invitation, Allamano had addressed him in deferential manner. They were still addressing one another in such manner forty-two years later.

The Pastoral Institute re-opens

While he set about organizing the Consolata (and even literally lending a hand with the cleaning), his problem remained the Pastoral Institute: not dead and not alive, not suppressed and not properly functioning. The young priests on the two-years course attended their lectures at the seminary but in an atmosphere of new quarrels spreading with ever more ferocious polemic through the parishes. It was not only a question of appointing this or that

40

teacher of Moral Theology, this or that assistant lecturer. The very Pastoral Institute itself, once the pride of the diocese, remained as it were confined in limbo, sterile in its creativity. There were indeed those who thought all this was the prelude to its suppression, and naturally held the Archbishop to blame: basically this Rosminian Gastaldi — the word ran — has always got it in for St Alphonsus, he wants to abolish his teaching and adopt a scorched earth policy with the Pastoral Institute, or turn it into something different and contrary to what Lanteri, Guala and Cafasso wanted it to be, what Bertagna went on keeping alive, and you know how he ended up. . .

Joseph Allamano, as we have seen, was appointed rector of the Consolata, of the Shrine of Sant'Ignazio at Lanzo, and also of the Pastoral Institute. So he had a primary responsibility and certain duties to intervene, in order to save the institution or at least to clear the matter up. And he did intervene with a letter his biographers regard as a document of capital importance, since it most completely mirrors what its author was made of, as priest and as man.

He was not one to grumble, and he never did grumble. Wherever he heard the Archbishop mentioned, he would immediately intervene to speak highly, very highly of him. He respected authority and had a lively esteem for the man. And so, he loved him; and was possibly one of the few who did, surrounding this very pugnacious and much attacked man. But, precisely for these reasons, he did not hide anything from him and did not mitigate the truth. The subdued voice that so impressed the seminarians, knew how to say distasteful things too.

He had already spoken to the Archbishop about returning the Pastoral Institute to the Consolata and getting it working properly again. But in July 1882, while he was at Sant'Ignazio, he tackled the question head-on by writing the famous letter which Giacomo Camisassa was to take to the Archbishop right-away.

In it, he begins by saying that among the Pastoral Institute's students there is a 'deep revulsion and despondency', which far from growing weaker is getting worse. 'I have spent much time reflecting on the causes of this discontent; and although I realize that ill-natured people ever ready to disparage any arrangement made by their superior have played a large part, I cannot however deny that there are other reasons too. . .' The Archbishop wants to appoint a theologian as professor who (in Moral Theology at least) seems little esteemed; Allamano advises against the appointment, proposing Agostino Richelmy (the future Archbishop of Turin) as an alternative. But then he moves on to the heart of the problem: the time has come to bring the Pastoral Institute back to the Consolata, both to put new life into the latter ('there is a shortage of priests at the Shrine to say Mass') and to make more room in the seminary for the students; but first and foremost to put an end to an ugly episode: 'Will the diocese not consider the Archbishop to have been justified by the event? The expulsion of the Pastoral Institute students from the Consolata four years ago was differently judged by the good and the ill-disposed. The latter will maliciously say that it stemmed from inveterate dislike of that institution and of St Alphonsus' teachings. The good, of whom there are many, even if not ignorant about the decay of the spirit of the Pastoral Institute, will nonetheless regard that measure as unduly severe, unless the abuses were so bad there was no other way of removing them. Others again, better informed and more enlightened, will regard a radical solution as the right one, but in the hope of soon seeing the Pastoral Institute reborn to new life.'

In a word, many people disapproved of the 'punishment' meted out to the Pastoral Institute; and if the story were to be further protracted, everyone would condemn it. And then: 'What better justification for the Archbishop than to demonstrate now by re-establishing the Pastoral Institute that in suppressing it he was not acting from unworthy motives but from the need to apply severe remedies appropriate to the gravity of the evils; which cured, he himself restores it to flourishing condition, transformed in accordance with his mind and the needs of the clergy? Would this not be clear proof of the honesty of his intentions and, while silencing the ill-disposed, confirm the expectations of the good?' In conclusion, he re-assures him about being frightened of losing face: 'Not even the superficial observer will be able to say that the Archbishop has made a

U-turn: since the final result will explain the previous actions and how these were all designed to prepare for its execution.'

'You have written me a letter. . . you have done well.' Archbishop Gastaldi was delighted by the thirty-one year old priest's frankness as well as by the arguments he set forth. Right! The Pastoral Institute shall rise again, but on one condition only: that the teacher of Moral Theology be none other than he, Collegiate Doctor Joseph Allamano.

The one condition is somewhat of a minefield, since it involves a chair that has already claimed illustrious victims: something like the 'siege perilous' of the Round Table in Camelot, waiting at Pentecost for 'its lord'. Joseph Allamano consents to sit in it because the Archbishop has made this the condition *sine qua non*, and because he is so anxious to re-establish the school and put an end to four disastrous years. And to restore to Turin, to the people of Turin who too have been deeply distracted, their favourite house of prayer and meeting-place; to bring the Consolata back to life.

So, on 6 November 1882, the Pastoral Institute resumes its activities in full at the Shrine, under the direction of Fr Allamano and his group of fellow-workers: Fr Luigi Fassini, Fr Giacomo Bertolone, Canon Ignazio Dematteis. And also of course Fr Giacomo Camisassa. The latter also becomes number two in the teaching of Moral Theology, as Allamano's 'assistant lecturer'.

Things are moving in the diocese of Turin. As early as 1874, the governmental *exequatur* (or approval) having at last been obtained, Archbishop Gastaldi was able to leave his temporary home in the seminary and move into the archiepiscopal palace. The Pastoral Institute too was now functioning in its proper place. And this meant that the Shrine of the Consolata came more alive since, because of the young priests of the Pastoral Institute, there could always be people on duty there. After the years of decline with the very small group of worn-out friars, the faithful found everything in working order again, celebrants for Mass, correct services, priests available to hear confessions or even merely to listen to those who want to confide and to give advice.

Turin had about 253,000 inhabitants at the end of 1881 (Milan had 321,000 and Rome 284,000) and could not yet be said to have recovered from the shock of no longer being the capital city. But there were signs of a new liveliness even so. Partly because the Italian situation had generally improved. From 1866 to 1880 the country had enjoyed its first period of peace, fourteen years, whereas the previous sixteen years had seen (for the Kingdom of Sardinia and Kingdom of Italy) three wars plus the Crimean expedition. Before falling in 1876, the ruling parties of the Right had balanced the national budget by successive bouts of taxation, confiscations, compulsory circulation of paper money. In 1880, the Cairoli-Depretis government was in a position finally to abolish the detested tax on ground cereals. Italy was still far from prosperous, as the emigration figures confirmed: from 1871 to 1880, 235,000 Italians went abroad, just about the population of Turin. But the spectre of imminent bankruptcy was at least dissolved, which had been an obsession for many years. Even the ruling classes' mistrust of the 'real country' diminished (by a little, a very little), to the extent that the risk was taken of very slightly extending the right to vote: from 2.2% of the population to 6.9%. In the political elections of 1882, the number of electors thus rose from 621,000 to more than 2 million. But as usual, abstention was rife: 800,000 non-voters.

Two lasting enterprises were founded in Turin in 1880: the Nebiolo letter-press factory and the National Steel factory of Savigliano; and in the decade 1871–1881 in Turin, the number of those employed in industry rose by 5%. As yet there was no entrepreneurial class properly speaking, but it was in the making with early attempts in every sort of direction. Initial mistakes, such as speculative building in Rome and elsewhere, ended in catastrophe. There was however a rich scientific and technical background, prepared in the very recent past by men like Germain Sommeiller and Carlo Ignazio Giulio and now represented by Galileo Ferraris of Vercelli, inventor of the rotating magnetic field motor, and by Alessandro Cruto of Piossasco, of the same age as Ferraris (both born 1847). Cruto perfected Edison's incandescent lamp by finding a method of strengthening the filaments. And in the Turin of 1881, experiments in lighting the streets by electricity were the result of this: at the Sub-Alpin Gallery and at the Porta Nuova railway station.

Before going to Vienna to enter into the Triple Alliance with the Emperor Franz Josef, King Umberto I visited Turin to lay the foundation stone of the new Mauriziano hospital. Horse-drawn trams were beginning to give way to ones propelled by steam. New churches too were being built. Three were consecrated in 1882: San Gioachino, San Giovanni Evangelista and San Secondo. The festivities for this last provoked fiery anti-clerical demonstrations, since Archbishop Gastaldi had planned it should also have a monument in honour of Pius IX: a statue of him was to be placed on the facade. Given the political climate, it was put up inside the church instead.

Making his rounds in the Shrine of the Consolata, Joseph Allamano too began thinking about new things. The time had come to change a lot even here. Permits, authorizations, money would be needed. But in the meantime the young rector began quietly laying his plans.

4

'I trust you'

So here was Joseph Allamano occupying the chair of Moral Theology at the Pastoral Institute. There were fifty-seven priest-students divided into two two-year courses. Some years later there would be even more. 'It was', people said, 'as though the days of Fr Cafasso had returned.'

Fr Cafasso. This ever mysterious uncle of whom he retains fleeting personal memories (the vague recollection of a childhood meeting, what his mother told him) now increasingly reveals himself to him, day by day, in the activities of the Pastoral Institute that had been so profoundly his. And principally in the teaching, in the subject of what he was generally remembered as a master: at every step his judgements and opinions were to be met with, he was constantly being quoted as an authority.

Joseph Allamano was not born a luminary of the lecture hall, any more than he was born a champion preacher. His true field was conversation, his instrument that soft voice at its most effective in a tête-à-tête but tending to get lost in the lecture hall or nave. Besides, he had a great many duties; the additional one of teaching came to him unexpectedly and certainly unsought. But now, there he was: having accepted out of obedience, he felt his duty was to do his best and committed himself to it with all his love for accurate preparation, planned lessons, notes, references to important authors. He taught that penitents were to be treated in the way laid down by Alphonsus de' Liguori, of course — and with the techniques of the day.

He was certainly in no position to revolutionize — himself being only a beginner at his age — the method of teaching Moral Theology, which consisted in posing a series of extremely subtle special cases to be resolved one by one. In the course of his teaching, he was never to be accused of laxism, as had happened to Bertagna to the Archbishop's great vexation; nonetheless he by no means toadied to the latter. It seems that, in accepting the post, he had said to the Archbishop: 'I obey, but I shall not use your treatises.' 'But I trust you', was the Archbishop's response. Afterwards, in truthfulness, he did decide to use those texts but had no intention of depending on them exclusively. Without regarding himself as an expert, he was seriously aware of the possible consequences of his way of teaching for future parish priests and confessors. Hence he stuck closely to Cafasso, who had trained so many fine ones. And as time goes by, it seems, he began to take pleasure in the work. At any rate, the Pastoral Institute students' protests ceased altogether, once he took over the job.

Archbishop Gastaldi had confidence in this thirty-year-old even in cases which would normally have been entrusted to old and experienced priests: those for instance of presumed evil possession. Allamano, in 1916, in his spiritual addresses to his missionaries recalled something that had happened in 1881: a woman from Loranzé in the diocese of Ivrea was sent to the Consolata by her bishop in the hope of seeing her freed from a 'diabolical obsession'. As she refused to enter the Shrine, Rector Allamano was asked to go and exorcize her in her lodgings. 'But I immediately replied: "I won't go!" Then word came from Archbishop Gastaldi, who sent to say that I was to go, at the same time to put new heart into those people; on which I went. The poor women showed all the signs of evil possession. And I shall tell you what those signs were. Scarcely had I gone in with a blessed medal of the Consolata than she flung herself at me and would have sprung on my back, if they had not held her tight. When I went in without anything, she was cheerful and took no notice, but when I went in with my stole, even when it was in my pocket, she instantly turned towards me and pointed me out to the bystanders, even when I was in a different room. I conducted quite a few tests, and she always turned to me when I had my stole, and if I did not have it, she took no more notice of my presence. If I went into her room without my stole, there was no reaction. But if I went in with my stole, even in my pocket, there was trouble. After a few tests, seeing that we could do nothing, we set to praying and performing the exorcisms with the stole; then she became irritated, emitting shouts and screams . . . She uttered insults and language such as I had never heard before in my life, nor shall ever hear again. . .' Eventually he tried another method: 'Taking the Consolata medal, I rushed into the room and placed it against her mouth, saying: "Acknowledge your Mistress!" That was it: she fell down like a dead woman! Then the others came and gave her some kind of restorative and she recovered her senses and gave grateful thanks to the Consolata and every year since has always come on pilgrimage to the Consolata to thank Our Lady. All this I saw with my own eyes . . . and this happened in the nineteenth century; these are facts and no one has ever found a natural explanation for them.'

The initial refusal ('I won't go!') was a sign of suspicion on his part, and Giacomo Camisassa adds that the Archbishop twice asked him to exorcise the woman from Loranzé, first by note and then by word of mouth. Then there were his tests: with stole, without stole, and finally the use of the medal. A series of actions which from one angle reveal him as sensitive to events and situations which are hard to discount — 'Some cases are merely frauds,' he often used to say, 'but there are genuine cases too.' — but it also reveals an argus-like caution in believing and letting others believe, in a period so prompt to involve the spirits whether to encourage faith or to combat it.

As we have already said, the Archbishop had also appointed him Rector of the Shrine of Sant'Ignazio at Lanzo, where cycles of retreats attracted crowds of priests and laymen every year. He had to superintend these gatherings. By now he was a key-figure in the diocesan structure that Archbishop Gastaldi had had such problems in assembling: a small group of new men, most of them in their thirties. Among them, with Allamano, there was Giuseppe Maria Soldati who had been put in charge of the Turin Metropolitan Seminary and Giuseppe Aniceto who carried out the Archbishop's plan of transforming the Archiepiscopal Institute at Giaveno into a seminary for boys, which was destined to become a most valuable nursery of new vocations.

There were those in the diocese who did not agree with these choices. Not with all of them at least, since no real objections were to be heard on Joseph Allamano's account. Others, in contrast, almost all undeservedly, were described as 'incompetent kids' by priests of undisputed authority. By now there was permanent dissension between one part of the clergy and the Archbishop. The latter, to cap it all, had to contend with failing health and with bouts of exhaustion that made it easier for him to make mistakes. Joseph Allamano saw him in these moments of weakness when calling on him. 'He was alone and he said to me: "I feel so depressed, I could cry all the time. The secretary has brought me some canaries to cheer me up, but instead they make me want to cry all the more." Then he added: "What? Am I going to cry? I certainly will not!" '

A great sign of his confidence in the rector of the Consolata: he was not afraid of letting him see him in this state, of confiding in him about these crises. Then, in a more serene moment, he decided to reward him for re-opening the Pastoral Institute by naming him honorary canon of Turin Cathedral. Honorary meant without pay, since the benefices which the chapter of canons used to enjoy had been harshly reduced by confiscations. The recognition however was significant on account of the youth of the new canon: the decree was issued in February 1883; Joseph Allamano was thirty-two.

But the moment for the final encounter between them arrived unexpectedly. On 24 March that year, on Easter Saturday, the Archbishop as always went to the Consolata to pray. Leaving with Allamano at his side, he glanced at the building: 'How nasty it looks!' Allamano replied that he already had a plan for restoring it and the Archbishop encouraged the idea: 'Then set to work! I began building the seminary at Giaveno when I hadn't a penny in my pocket; I spent one hundred thousand lire and don't owe a penny to anyone.' They agreed that Allamano should sign the work contract that very following Monday and lunch with the Archbishop on Tuesday. In any case they would see each other next morning at pontifical High Mass in the cathedral, when Allamano was to make his first appearance wearing his canon's cape.

Instead, next morning, Easter Sunday 1883, the secretary found the Archbishop in a state of unconsciousness on the floor at 7.30 a.m., and little more than two hours later he was dead. 'The city of Turin, its people and authorities, shared unanimously in the diocese's mourning. On the morning of Wednesday 28 March, between throngs of people lining the streets, estimated at 150,000 persons, the Archbishop was escorted to his cathedral church for the last farewell. It is said that so many people had never been seen since the funeral of Queen Maria Adelaide' (G. Tuninetti). Triumphal honours, as it were, after eleven years of very troubled government.

So they never did see each other again at Mass or over lunch, he and Joseph Allamano, but the latter kept his word given on Holy Saturday: on Easter Monday he signed the contract for the restoration of the Shrine. The works were to last for two years, at a cost of 125,000 lire. And Fr Tubaldo summarizes them thus: 'The restoration work, starting with the outside, was entrusted to the architect G. B. Ferrante. Without alteration to the original lines imposed on the building by Guarini and Juvara, the great cupola was freed of an ungainly gallery encircling it; the spurs projecting from the lower roofs were also eliminated; the capitals and the lower parts of the drum of the cupola as well as other external surfaces were refaced in stone; the state of the gallery overlooking the Church of Sant'Andrea was overhauled; a massive stone plinth was applied round the entire outside perimeter of the Shrine; and the entire complex was girdled with iron railings. Further necessary and costly restoration included covering the cupola and roofs with lead and replacing the tiles with slabs of stone.'

Arrival of the Cardinal

Eight months after Archbishop Lorenzo Gastaldi's death, Turin received its new archbishop. He was not a Piedmontese, not even a bishop promoted to Turin from some other sub-Alpine diocese, as had been the case on other occasions. This time, the Holy See sent a Cardinal from Rome, a member of the Curia. He was a Ligurian, Gaetano

Alimonda, previously Bishop of Albenga, sixty-five years of age, a very famous orator (he was to leave twelve volumes of sermons at his death). In Rome he was often called on to speak in the name and even instead of the Pope, whenever Leo XIII felt he should not lay himself open to criticism in person. He was already old beyond his years, had a mild disposition and an absolute horror of conflict.

To receive an Archbishop who was also a Cardinal was a rare honour for the diocese, which in those days did not enjoy Cardinal status. But the totally Roman stamp of the appointment gave it the look of a commission of investigation or something of the sort. It heralded radical changes, purges. And as such, various members of the Turinese clergy hastened to interpret it, immediately ready to give the peace-loving Gaetano Alimonda a hard time even before he arrived. Advice, suggestions, insinuations from all sides: even to the point of insult, as when the well-known journalist Fr Margotti tried to explain to him how he should conduct himself towards King Umberto. The result could be foreseen: the new Archbishop arrived in Turin, completely disinformed and stuffed up with prejudice against 'Gastaldi's men', who had been depicted to him as sinks of iniquity. (His arrival in his diocese on 18 November 1883, was a simple affair, not a solemn entry. A closed carriage as far as the cathedral and then, in the brief climb up the steps, shouts and whistles from the square, obliging him later to leave the building by another door.)

New (or, rather, old) faces in the Archbishop's palace. The Cardinal allowed himself to be piloted, partly owing to his good-natured temperament, partly owing to fatigue. He accepted things in the way they were presented to him — to start with, at least — with little inclination to see and verify for himself. (At a certain point he was to discover to his amazement that the little country town of Carmagnola belonged to his diocese; he had no idea.)

The most sensational happening in the new scheme of things was an overdue act of reparation. Mgr Bertagna, whom Archbishop Gastaldi had abruptly dismissed, was recalled with full honours from Asti where he was the vicar general. On 1 May 1884, Cardinal Alimonda consecrated him bishop, appointing him as his auxiliary, and also put him in charge of all the seminaries. This in turn entailed the dismissal of Soldati, the rector of the metropolitan seminary, whom certain persons accused of excessive 'Gastaldian' harshness. But the method adopted for removing him was still unacceptable, and he found it more than he could bear, scarcely surviving it by two years. It fell to Joseph Allamano to comfort him a little, in the course of many meetings at the Consolata.

And what of Allamano himself?

At one time it looked as though he would be the last of Gastaldi's men to remain in office. Among the priests now habitual visitors at the Archbishop's palace — Cardinal Alimonda, the soul of cordiality, entertained a great many of them to lunch or dinner — who knows how many names were canvassed to succeed him in his various posts: at the Consolata, at Sant'Ignazio, at the Pastoral Institute. . .

Instead something happened that the Archbishop had certainly not decreed. It fell out that Bishop Bertagna reappeared at the Pastoral Institute and in his new capacity began talking to the students on topics of moral theology. At a certain point these conversations turned into lectures; they became regular. . . somehow. And thus the teaching was taken out of Allamano's hands by a *de facto* occupation of his chair, without anyone's having decided this should happen. And Cardinal Alimonda eventually learned of it as a *fait accompli*, with amazement bordering on consternation.

But for the moment nothing more happened. Joseph Allamano pursued his own life in the background; and this had already happened before. He said nothing, and with the low profile he favoured followed the exterior restoration work on the Consolata day by day. The work when completed was to cost 125,000 lire, and part of this he met from his own pocket (40,000 lire, apparently); then there were some outstandingly large contributions: from the royal family even. But the little miracle of the restoration work lay in the fact that the greater part of the cost was defrayed by thousands and thousands of tiny offerings, lire and cents: it was the Turinese population that provided for its Shrine, putting its trust in this rector with his smile so mild and his voice so meek, who had brought warmth and life back

52

under those vaults. The people had already been on his side when he appealed for help in dealing with the external structure.

The rector was also thinking about the inside. Here, too, much needed changing. But for the moment, the initial efforts to preserve and make good would have to do, since they had to be finished by 1885. That year it was intended to celebrate the fiftieth anniversary of recourse to the Consolata in the cholera epidemic, commemorated on the votive column erected near the Shrine.

Meanwhile Turin witnessed great celebrations of another kind in 1884: the National Exhibition was held there and for the first time the political ex-capital presented itself to the Italian nation in the guise, still barely fleshed out, of a capital of industry. A stage between past and future. On this occasion, Edmondo De Amicis sided with the past. For him, the most attractive aspects of Turin were those festivities bringing back figures of the past to the banks of the River Po: '. . . elderly ministers who have spent the best of their mature years here, mature deputies who have spent the best years of their youth here, journalists who first cut their teeth here, rich men who used to be poor here. . . all have thousands of memories here. . .' At the Exhibition however, the accent was on the future. Represented, for example, by electric current, now usable not only for lighting but as industrial power; with transformers, the problem of how to transport it was on the way to being solved; and in fact the power for lighting the pavilion came from Lanzo. And then there was the future already present in the person of Francesco Cirio, for instance. For the occasion, Carlo Anfosso wrote: 'Signor Cirio began his tinned vegetable industry with his special methods of conservation, here in Turin; the cheapness of these Italian products and the absolutely safe way in which they are preserved now put them within the budget of the less wealthy, whereas these canned foods were previously reserved only for the most sumptuous tables.'

The concluding day of the festivities in 1885 was 20 June, a Saturday. At the Consolata, there were Mass and sermon by the Cardinal in the morning, procession in the afternoon. But in some newspapers, including the *Gazzetta del Popolo*, there appeared an 'anti-clerical proclamation by the democratic associations', in which the imminent procession at the Consolata was described as follows: 'Saturday, 20 June at 6 o'clock in the afternoon, on the pretext of a festival dedicated to the crudest superstitious worship, the leftovers from old pagan idolatry (the clericals) intend making our Turin a theatre for their stupid outbursts of fanaticism. . .' An explicit invitation followed for a rough-house intervention to wreck the procession. Shortly afterwards, on 17 June, the chief of police Bartolomeo Casalis issued a decree: 'The religious procession in the parish of the Consolata is forbidden, as is any other display or religious demonstration outside the precincts of the said church.' Cardinal Alimonda reacted to this with a communication which in substance said: since the Consolata could not visit the Turinese in their streets, the Turinese should come and visit the Consolata in her church. Hence, owing to the anti-clerical proclamation, the chief of police's decree and the Archbishop's invitation, the result was such a crowd as had never been seen in the Shrine — all day long.

'And I resign'

'It seems that the new Archbishop had to some degree been prejudiced against the Turinese clergy, under the impression that they had sympathies, if not with Jansenism, then at least with rigorism. He was therefore prejudiced against many members of the clergy, among whom was Fr Allamano.' Thus runs one piece of testimony given at his canonical process. And Allamano became aware of this on his first contact with the new Archbishop and his new entourage. As he saw Gastaldi's former collaborators one by one being removed from their posts, he felt that his own turn would be coming too. Even if being labelled a Jansenist or a rigorist must have seemed rather odd to him as Cafasso's nephew and what was more as his convinced continuator at the Pastoral Institute.

But it seems that among the many frequenters of the archbishop's palace, someone must have whispered into the right ears an accusation not about doctrine but about money.

54

In a word, that there might be doubt over Joseph Allamano's honesty in his administration of the Shrine.

And so — probably at about the end of the restorations — an invitation arrived from the Archbishop to present the complete accounts for the Consolata. Which he immediately did, since his 'exactness' would not tolerate arrears and every figure was immediately entered, each item of income and expenditure recorded. And from the Archbishop, these impeccable accounts were then sent back to him — in silence however, without comment or message of any sort. At this, the outraged integrity of the man from Monferrato rose to the surface in the charming honorary canon of Turin Cathedral. Already when sending the accounts to the Archbishop, he had explained to him in a letter that he was ready to leave forthwith, on the understanding of course that if so the Curia would meet the outstanding debts. Afterwards, that is to say, almost immediately after the accounts had been returned to him in that way, he decided that he would say something, even if the Archbishop did not; he would go in person to the Cardinal and hand in his resignation.

But he never got as far as the archbishop's palace, having run into Fr Felice Carpignano of the Oratorians, a gem of the Piedmontese clergy and one of the consciences of Turin. He was confessor to a great many people, starting with Prince Amadeus the ex-King of Spain, and had also been Archbishop Gastaldi's. He was Joseph Allamano's confessor too. It was Fr Felice who stopped him: he was not to resign but go back to the Consolata and get on with his work.

He obeyed, went back and waited. But from the shore, he was not to see the corpses of his enemies floating down river. Better, far better: he was to see the man whom he took to be his most powerful persecutor come sailing into port as his friend: Cardinal Gaetano Alimonda in person. Light was breaking in on this honest but misdirected man. He had begun to get a different view of things when visiting the dying Canon Soldati, who had been so unjustly removed from the seminary. And he demonstrated this by a concrete gesture: Canon Soldati had been superior of the Josephite Sisters of Turin and the Archbishop appointed Soldati's friend Allamano to be his successor. So he had reason to think that suspicions might be fading away. Perhaps the appointment was a sign of this. However, a definite reply came later, publicly, when the Archbishop, in front of the canons of the cathedral, said to him: 'They misled me about you.' And embraced him, according to Fr Sales. According to Canon Nicola Baravalle, however, 'he made to embrace him but Allamano discreetly avoided it.'

Reassured, he went on with the work. Anticipating a little, we shall now see him engaged in the second building operation: beautifying the interior of the Shrine of the Consolata and making it larger from inside. The financial proportions of the undertaking were enormous this time; a million lire was mentioned as the figure. And the technical problems were of discouraging complexity. However he went ahead. To shoulder the cost, Canon Allamano counted on the people of Turin and, to solve the building problems on Fr Giacomo Camisassa.

And now the vice rector came into his own, with his competence and his passion for craftsmanship, completely at ease with blacksmiths, masons, carpenters. It was he who insisted so firmly on the need to make the Shrine larger still, when it was already being enlarged. He had already worked out how to do it, and he explained how to the great architect, Count Carlo Ceppi, who was consulted over the undertaking: 'My lord Count, until 1706 the altar stood below the large arch of the balustrade and Juvara, to please Victor Amadeus II, took the wall down, and you can see what a magnificent enlargement that made! Like him, why don't we do the same sort of thing by throwing out chapels round the sides?' The architect agreed: 'You open a glimmer of light for me where all was dark before.'

Work began in 1898 and Fr Camisassa was man-of-all-trades, assistant, paymaster, inspector. He weighed and measured everything, negotiated with the suppliers, but then starting meddling with the work and workmen too: which was no concern of his. And one fine day, Count Ceppi left. The architect Giovanni Battista Ferrante took over from him and the story ended in the same way. Sparks flew continually and it needed all Fr Allamano's patience to make peace between them by saving first one man's face and then the other's. The architect Antonio Vandone was eventually to complete the works: to him in particular was due the decoration of the interior with a profusion of multi-coloured marble, which was to astonish visitors from 1904 onwards. For these had been used to surroundings blackened by time and candle-smoke, stone floors, and walls peeling off in patches.

Of this joyful astonishment, Fr Sales stands interpreter: 'The Shrine of the Consolata is now truly lovely. The Church of Sant'Andrea, with its marbles shown off to great effect by the gilding, and the marvellous gilded stucco vaulting that puts new life into the ancient paintings, with the three flights of steps leading up to the Shrine looks like the magnificent vestibule of a royal palace. . . The Shrine, like a pearl in a golden setting, is surrounded inside by the imposing circle of the four new chapels supported by a forest of marble columns, rich in air and light, blazing with gold, smiling in spring-time freshness with the elegant medallions in the small cupola, painted by Morgari. . .'

The costs were gradually covered, as the first time, by some large contributions (even from the municipality of Turin) and tens of thousands of tiny payments; popular support once again solved the problem, due to the general attachment to the Consolata. Due also to the rector. He had started a monthly newsletter called *La Consolata*, through which he issued invitations, provided information and notices about the state of the works, and estimates. One is struck by the remarkable sobriety of the appeals — an elegant request, in the true Allamano style. For in one of the newsletters for 1901 we read: 'Out of a right and proper sense of discretion, we have not so far approached any wealthy people to ask for contributions, for it has not been, nor will it be, our method to voice day after day the need of having them in order to keep on with the works. The Servant of God, Fr Joseph Cafasso, our venerated predecessor and master in the governing of the Pastoral Institute, did not approve of using moral coercion as a means of achieving good works, but preferred, following the Venerable Cottolengo's example, to rely on people's spontaneous generosity.'

Among the thousands of contributions there was one in 1893 from a young married woman who brought an *ex-voto* offering to the altar of the Shrine for favours received:

one of very, very many, but perhaps the first of its kind. The young woman had married a captain 'aeronaut and aerostat builder' in Turin on 8 October. The honeymoon trip took place actually in an aerostat, first from Turin to Piobesi and then towards the mountains, where however the balloon was smashed to pieces and her husband lost his life in a crevasse, while she and two other passengers were saved.

It was also to be remembered later that in the Shrine — before, during and after the process of transformation — he himself was always at work as minister of the sacrament of reconciliation. Those endless hours in the confessional, that plaintive, untiring voice, ever there to extend trust, to orientate, to rebuild Christians. . . Here Joseph Allamano truly was and meant to be the leading figure. But he played little part in the solemn services, willingly leaving the principal role to others. All the same, he cared very much for every aspect of liturgical activity, with a preparation even pedantic but entirely geared to making the faithful aware of what was going on and of taking their part in it. For this reason he was demanding with celebrants even in very minor matters: 'Human beings are material and earthly; in order to perceive the divine presence in our houses, they observe how we ourselves behave. If we do not behave faithfully, they will not manage to see heavenly things here.'

Fr Cafasso is here

In Joseph Allamano's life as rector of the Pastoral Institute, there was one moment that recurred every year for years, a special moment: it was when, the two-year course of moral theology completed, he informed each young priest of his first appointment: 'You will go as junior curate to. . .' In a sense it was he who presented the Church of Turin with new priests for the care of souls, guaranteeing for each one of them and for all.

Training priests. This was always to be his primary task. They might be destined for parishes in Turin, for the sub-Alpine countryside or for the plains of Africa. He was aware of the huge responsibility involved but without fear, or doubts of making mistakes, or scruples: as a stimulus rather. And it was he, furthermore, who put an end in the Pastoral Institute to the long standing conflict between severity and mercy. And the man who helped him was ever that dead man who day by day became more present in his life: Giuseppe Cafasso. At the Pastoral Institute, especially when teaching, he had been able to complete his discovery of him and deepen his own teaching. To train good priests, one had to learn his lesson. Or better still: present him in entirety to young priests as a living model; the notes on his lessons and the comments on his writings were not enough.

From that Allamano conceived the idea of exploring the life of Fr Giuseppe Cafasso in depth and writing it; and also to taking the first steps on a canonical itinerary with a view to his perhaps being raised to the altars.

No precise date for these decisions, maturing deep inside him, is known. We do however know that he had recourse to another priest in Turin for advice and help; the latter had been grateful to Fr Cafasso all his life: Don Bosco. He had every reason to remember Fr Cafasso's refusals which closed off a path but opened a street for him; no to the idea of becoming a junior curate or a tutor; no to the idea of becoming a missionary; but yes to working among the wild boys of Turin.

When Joseph Allamano went to see him, Don Bosco must already have been near death. He had fulfilled the mission given him by Leo XIII (task? test? penance?) of finding the money in Italy and the rest of Europe for the Church of the Sacred Heart in Rome. He had been to take part, worn out, in the celebrations of priests and boys of his Spanish institutes.

Back in the 1860s, Don Bosco had always commemorated Fr Cafasso in his periodical, *Letture Cattoliche*, also announcing the future publication of a biography of him; but this never appeared. Now, at the final stage of his life, he explained to Joseph Allamano why the book had not been written: 'They took the documents away from me and then I didn't know anything more about him. But you can put this right. . .' And he advised him to send out circular letters asking for information and statements about Giuseppe Cafasso. This was just what Allamano did as he later handed over the assembled material to the person assigned to write the biography: Giacomo Colombero, the then rector of the seminary at Chieri and future parish priest of Santa Barbara in Turin. After a troubled progress, the work appeared in 1895.

Later the rector of the Consolata was to put the learned Fr Luigi Nicolis di Robilant to work on a more complete, definitive biography. The two thick volumes appeared posthumously in 1911–1912, the author having died in 1904. But as regards the biographies, Joseph Allamano had not confined himself to procuring documents and statements and letting things go at that. He too had worked constantly on these materials with the help of Giacomo Camisassa. Who can tell? — perhaps he did not foresee how totally he would be taken over by this presence, by means of testimonies and reminiscences that made Fr Cafasso come alive in what he said and what he did, to his nephew at the Consolata. And in essence it would be like that for the rest of his life and whatever else he was doing.

On 16 February 1895, he completed the first official step in the long, canonical *iter*, by asking for an ordinary diocesan investigation to be started. This would first have to make sure about Fr Cafasso's reputation for holiness, and then carry on to an examination of his life and virtues. Fr Giacomo Bertolone, bursar of the Consolata, was appointed as postulator of the cause. But he, a year later, while reading his breviary in the confessional, had vitriol thrown in his face and was practically blinded by a woman of easy virtue. He was replaced by Giacomo Boccardo, who had recently been appointed vice rector of the Pastoral Institute.

In the meantime, Fr Giuseppe Cafasso's remains had been transferred from Turin cemetery to the Shrine of the Consolata. And his *Meditations* and his *Instructions* for the clergy were printed and put into circulation, published in 1892 and 1893 respectively by Joseph Allamano.

When the diocesan investigation opened, Joseph Allamano was called as first witness by the postulator of the cause, starting on 8 February 1897. An interrogation which, in various sessions until the next November, reconstructed Fr Cafasso's life, as he was more than qualified to do from having read hundreds of documents, letters, statements, registers. In his youth he had tried to write his uncle's biography. But the real biography was the one he traced before the diocesan commission, in telling, in answering questions and objections, in offering proofs and confirmations. His 'discovery' of Fr Cafasso was extraordinarily enriched by this investigation, and even led to 'revelations' concerning himself, Joseph Allamano. For instance, when he recognized himself in his uncle's very insistent care for precision and dignity in the liturgy and in the attitude of young priests at the altar; or when, in him, he saw that same attachment to discipline ('very attentive in procuring it') accompanied by 'gentle' methods of having it respected — just like his own 'I'm sorry' murmured in his soft voice, which the student thus rebuked remembered for months. Or again: giving evidence on Fr Cafasso's lessons at the Pastoral Institute, he emphasized that the Alphonsian doctrine was in no way 'accommodated', but rather expounded with rigorous fidelity, but also 'mildly and kindly'. Here too uncle and nephew were to be found in agreement. In a word, Joseph Allamano must have had some startling surprises every time he realized he had been acting, speaking and thinking like him without knowing, even before reading all that testimony.

In his statement, much is said about Fr Cafasso as comforter of those condemned to death: 'the priest of the gallows', as the Turinese used to call him. It is recorded that all whom he assisted died with signs of repentance and reconciliation. The words of an executioner are quoted: 'At Fr Cafasso's presence, death is no longer death but a joy, a comfort, a pleasure.' To assist condemned men on that last night, to accompany them to the scaffold, was a terrible experience which few priests found themselves strong enough to face. Even Don Bosco, who once accompanied Fr Cafasso to a double execution at Alessandria, fell down in a faint at the sight of the gallows.

While doing his best for the diocesan cause, he took care to keep Giuseppe Cafasso's memory green among the people, with words and even pictures, with a well-developed grasp of mass communication; as early as 1894, he was at pains to get portraits of him made and printed. And in a year he was to do the same with the picture of the Consolata, distributing an excellent reproduction in Italy and then all over the world. This obtained one exceptional devotee for her: the Turinese lawyer Secondo Pia, to whom we owe the first photographic reproduction of the Shroud.

5

Waiting for ten years

In December 1887-January 1888, Joseph Allamano made
a sort of brief tour of Italy lasting about five weeks: his
longest journey. The occasion was the first jubilee of Leo
XIII, that of fifty years in the priesthood. Cardinal Alimonda in his rounded rhetoric had invited the faithful to make
the pilgrimage to Rome, to demonstrate that there was no
coldness in Piedmont towards the pontiff: 'At the foot of
the Alps, on the banks of its many rivers, of which the principal one is the Po, it is not true that Piedmont harbours
cold, slow, insensitive souls: the eternal ice may clothe the
heights of the Lepontine and Pennine, Graian and Cottian
Alps: in the vale and on the plain, there is warmth enough
for great and vital actions. . .'

He took advantage of this pilgrimage to make a series
of short visits, stopping on the way out at Milan, Padua,
Venice, Bologna, Loreto, Assisi and Foligno. On his return,
he was to press on as far as Naples, Pompei and
Montecassino, before making further stops at Pisa, Florence
and Genoa. In Rome he attended the very solemn jubilee
Mass on 1 January 1888; it was the first time since 1870 that
a Pope had celebrated at the Altar of the *Confessio* and he
was surrounded by delegations and diplomatic missions sent
by governments the world over. But there was no one to
represent the Kingdom of Italy. The Crispi government had
however sent infantry and *bersaglieri* — as it were on tacit
loan — to keep order in St Peter's Square and regulate the
flow at the basilica.

On 11 January, he attended the 5 o'clock general audience
for the North Italian pilgrims and, together with scores of
others, was briskly presented to the Pope. In his diary he
noted down what Leo XIII had said to him, referring to
the Consolata and the Pastoral Institute: 'Good, very good,

that Shrine. . . Yes, I give a special blessing; tell them to study hard.' In all, that was the audience; there were thousands of other people.

In Rome he then called on many important persons, among whom the Prefect and the Secretary of Propaganda Fide, Cardinal Simeoni and Mgr Jacobini, attracted his special attention; and Guglielmo Massaia, the legendary missionary. Having spent thirty-five adventurous years as Bishop and Cardinal in Ethiopia, he was now living in a convent with his brother Capuchins. To this fellow-countryman of his from Asti and the two top men of the missionary congregation, would Joseph Allamano have mentioned a project of his own in that direction?

We have no evidence either way, but certain it is he had had a plan in his mind for some time: to create an Institute in Turin, a specialized school, to collect pupils from the numerous Piedmontese clergy and train them for the missions, then putting them at the disposal of Propaganda Fide for them to be employed where needed.

He had drawn his inspiration for this idea from a Genoese enterprise: the Ecclesiastical College for Foreign Missions, founded by Marquis Antonio Brignole-Sale. But the original impetus came from much further away. Here he found himself linking up with figures like Fr Diessbach, with the evangelistic thrust of his Christian Fellowships; and with his successor Pio Brunone Lanteri, master of the Oblates of the Virgin Mary who were to get as far as Burma, he being personally charged in the days of the Restoration with sending missionaries to the United States. This vocation had been inherited by Luigi Guala's Pastoral Institute, shortly after the return of the large missionary organizations to the scene: the Congregation of Propaganda Fide, reorganized in 1817; the Society of Jesus, reconstituted in 1815. Sign of and support for this resumption of missionary work was the founding at Lyon in the 1820s of the Work for the Propagation of the Faith, gradually spreading throughout Europe down to village level. A new institution in the history of the Church, since administered by the laity. Their task was to collect and distribute funds for the missions, by making the Catholic world aware of the problems of evangelization by means of widely circulated publications.

The missionary annals of the Work for the Propagation of the Faith had been read regularly for years at the Pastoral Institute, on Fr Cafasso's orders. He himself was a member of the Work, one of the earliest in Turin. Alphonsus de' Liguori's moral theology was taught in the Pastoral Institute and it hardly seems rash to think that popular works were also known there, such as the history of the martyrs of Japan, a heroic and tragic event bridging the sixteenth and seventeenth centuries, with missionaries and converts crucified on a hillside near Nagasaki; it was a very well-known work in the colleges and seminaries of the eighteenth century and nourished, among other things, the missionary vocation of Daniel Comboni. Lastly, from Fr Cafasso's private correspondence we find that he also helped individual missionaries, directly and discreetly, out of his own pocket.

In a word, Joseph Allamano also rediscovered his uncle here, in the mission field, where again he seemed to have left tracks and signposts for him.

Then there had been the great missionary activist in Turin, Canon Giuseppe Ortalda, who died in 1880. As local director of the Work for the Propagation of the Faith, he collected funds in growing quantity by publications, exhibitions and lotteries, eventually managing to found 'the apostolic schools' for training missionaries. At least this was the intention. But rich in enthusiasm and talents as he was, he lacked the necessary administrative experience. He found no one to help him in this very uncertain business, and the works he succeeded in bringing into existence were not properly supervised afterwards.

Other schemes, some of them on a smaller scale and always better supported, did however take root and survive. Since 1871 some Sisters of St Anne, sent by Mother Enrichetta Dominici, had been at work in the Vicariate Apostolic of Hyderabad, India. In 1875, Giovanni Cagliero had led the first Salesian missionary expedition to Patagonia.

So he already had something in mind before his pilgrimage to Rome at the end of 1887. Besides, many a time he had seen first the seminarians, then the young priests, pawing the ground at the prospect of becoming missionaries: many of them dreamed of this adventure rather than of being junior curates. But not all the bishops were pleased at the prospect of seeing them leave. Supporting the missions: an excellent thing to do, and indeed the bishops spared no efforts in this direction; but to keep supplying them with men — this was not so pleasant. There was fear of seeing a scarcity of clergy, although some important parishes were served by as many as ten priests.

The first document

Nothing happened — nothing is documented — before the April of 1891. On 6 April, a Monday, Joseph Allamano wrote a long letter to Fr Calcedonio Mancini, a Lazarist (Congregation of the Mission), on the advice of another Lazarist working in Turin, Fr Giovanni Tasso. The letter was an invitation to sound out the Congregation of Propaganda Fide as to how the idea might be received for 'a regional Institute for priests devoted exclusively to the missions, to which they could go as a homogeneous unit, in a specific area, under their own superiors.'

So, we are no longer at the Brignole-Sale type of institute, training priests and then handing them on to Propaganda Fide. The project is a completely new one, for which the personnel is already available: 'Even today I have a certain number of priests (and laymen will not be lacking) who have recently finished their training: young men of good conduct, full of promise, by whom, once having let them glimpse the hope of starting a regional Missionary Institute, I am daily besieged with requests to undertake this work; they being ready to devote themselves at once with energy and zeal, of which some have already given proof in the exercise of the sacred ministry.'

It is therefore a question of finding out whether, in principle, Propaganda Fide 'would welcome this attempt', given that he, Joseph Allamano, had already selected the future missionaries' field of action: a region in East Africa which the letter describes in considerable detail for the Vatican Congregation's information. Clearly he must have been working on this for a long time, since he had already given thought to other things as well: 'As regards the organization of this work, I have already drafted a complete plan, which I can present at any time. To mention the essentials: the priests and seculars, after sufficient testing and preparation in a suitable house in Turin, will engage to stay in the missions for five years, obeying their own superior and bound by the usual vows as in religious congregations. At the end of that time, either they will renew their vows for a further five years or return to their diocese under the authority of their Bishop. After ten years in the missions they may be admitted to perpetual vows or may continue in temporary vows. For those who go home, the Institute will provide for their maintenance until they receive a suitable post from their Bishop; and those bound by perpetual vows will always be a charge on the Institute. As regards the finances, I put my trust in the charity of the public and already have promises for as much as would be needed to begin.'

At this point Allamano stresses again that it is a question of first finding out what Propaganda Fide's attitude may be, and not of a formal request for recognition: 'and this is why I have not yet spoken of this to our Most Venerated Cardinal Archbishop, sure as I am of having approval and support for the scheme as soon as I mention it to him.' So he had as yet said nothing to Cardinal Alimonda and of course would not do so until some sign of approval in general terms were to arrive.

Approval of it came right away, with a speed that would have been astonishing in the Vatican of a hundred years later. On 13 April, Fr Mancini was already informing Allamano through Fr Tasso that 'the project has made a very good impression and been received with satisfaction.' There was one problem however about where the mission was to be, but that could be resolved at a personal meeting in Rome where the rector of the Consolata 'will find all support and favour'.

He for his part replied as promptly, on 17 April, saying that before going to Rome he would have to inform the Archbishop, now that there was initial approval; and to put him properly in the picture, he would also have to know 'in which area the difficulties lie' with regard to the placing of the mission. At the same time he also wrote to Cardinal Alimonda, who was sick in Genoa, explaining the facts to him. Here we do not have the exchange of letters, but by indirect means one thing becomes quite clear: that the Archbishop of Turin was not at all pleased about the approach to Rome, about this sounding of Propaganda Fide. In fact a number of days went by in silence, then a letter arrived from the secretary in Genoa, informing him that, owing to illness, the Cardinal could not deal with 'the business'.

While another invitation to discuss the matter in person arrived from the Vatican, Joseph Allamano and Giacomo Camisassa, who worked as a team, had to reply that the Archbishop's opposition made the journey to Rome impossible. Or perhaps, rather than the Archbishop, someone in his entourage was opposed to the scheme and keen to sabotage it in every way. This was what Fr Camisassa wrote to Fr Barbagli, procurator of the Congregation for Missions in Rome, who had pressed for Allamano's visit. So instead, if Propaganda Fide thought Allamano's project such a good thing, it should itself 'in some way or other express to our Archbishop the desire of seeing it realized', at the same time giving Canon Allamano a direct and open approval for his project 'and assuring him of protection and moral support in carrying it out.' We cannot leave here against the wishes of our Bishop, Camisassa is saying, in a word, but if you help us, then no one will be able to stop us. 'Certainly the work, once well begun, will then go forward under its own momentum, even though similar problems will arise later; but if at the outset there is friction with local superiors, it will be as it were stifled at birth and not take root either in this or any other diocese. For the rest, I repeat, do not stop giving me advice. . . the work is possible and, given the temperament of the Piedmontese clergy, it seems that with the help of God, it will do much good. . . and then. . .' In a word: allow us to start, and then you will see.

But so much realism and so much straightforwardness were useless, for on 30 May Cardinal Alimonda died in Genoa, aged seventy-three.

At this point there was no more talk of going to Rome. Everything had to be shelved while they waited for the new Archbishop, and waited for him without much hope, as Allamano wrote on 22 July to Fr Barbagli: 'Can I be sure the new Archbishop will understand it properly and consequently know how to stand firm against the gossiping of those who, by complaining about this reduction of the clergy, will try to arouse the opposition of the Archbishop against me?'

His own thought goes out to the world to be evangelized. But other people cannot see beyond the presbytery door. And the sad thing is that we are not talking about treacherous people waging war on him; they are good people, honest churchmen who take no steps against him, but merely oppose him with the static energy of their shortsightedness and petty fears. The idea of having one junior curate less affects them more than the anguish for the millions of people in the world still living in ignorance of Christ. True, even for them, this is a very sad situation, so much so that they collect money for the missions, sometimes even diverting it from their own parochial needs. But to let priests leave, this is quite unacceptable, it would be undermining the diocese. As Camisassa perceptively wrote to Rome: '. . . Canon Allamano has been accused of, as it were, taking advantage of his position to attract young priests, to the detriment of the diocese.'

Hence they had to submit and keep quiet. To wait for the new Archbishop but without any illusions, since the arguments of the fearful ones might influence him too, as had been the case with poor Cardinal Alimonda: how could one complain about his refusal to approve, once one knew he had gone to Genoa with a liver tumour and died after an operation performed without anaesthetic? Joseph Allamano was in the dilemma of knowing himself to be right, yet of having no means of persuading those who were wrong. He gave up all idea of going to Rome; in September 1891, at the request of Cardinal Simeoni, prefect of Propaganda Fide, he sent him the overall plan for the Missionary Institute. But he stressed that he did not intend doing anything before knowing, and absolutely clearly, whether the new Archbishop of Turin approved of his idea. For the time being, he was happy that someone so highly placed as Cardinal Simeoni should value the scheme.

But the trial went on: Cardinal Simeoni died of pneumonia in January 1892, aged seventy-six. Cardinal Miecislaus Ledòchowski became head of Propaganda Fide: a Pole, an apostolic nuncio, then a Bishop in his native land but under Prussian rule. Defender of the Pope during the conflict with the German Empire, he was imprisoned by Bismarck and while actually in prison was nominated Cardinal by Leo XIII. A splendid figure, a witness to the faith. However, on receiving Giacomo Camisassa in Rome, he said Allamano's plan was of no interest 'since he said there are more than enough missionary institutes in Italy.'

And what of the young priests of the Pastoral Institute who were constantly pawing the ground? He kept them quiet, of course; his soft voice would never encourage impatience or instil yearnings for the new. Meanwhile he singled out those among them who showed the most genuine aptitude for missionary work and saw to it that they did not become disheartened. In other words, to use his own words, he went on 'training those priests in the spirit of their vocation, who wanted to devote themselves to this work.'

And nor did he for his part offer any gesture or word of impatience. He did not find himself short of support, since in his discomfort as always his beloved *Imitation of Christ* came to his rescue, there precisely where it speaks of patience: 'You are not truly patient if you will only endure what you think fit, and only from those whom you like. A truly patient man does not consider by whom he is tried, whether by his superior, his equal, or his inferior; whether by a good and holy man, or by a perverse and wicked one. . .' (III, 19, 1).

The *Imitation*, Joseph Allamano always used to say, should be read in short passages, and each of these needed then to be meditated on at length. He however used a special expression: to *ruminate* on those words, as cattle slowly chew the cud. The time for ruminating on the theme of patience now began for him and was to last ten years.

The new Archbishop

He waited in silence but certainly not in inactivity. Be it remembered that he was still rector of the Pastoral Institute where, since 1886, he had had Fr Luigi Boccardo to help him. Fr Boccardo then became spiritual director, thus lightening his workload further. He was still dealing with the Shrine of Sant'Ignazio and the retreats connected with it. And then, as rector of the Consolata, he had to divide his time between the huge building programme that was to transform the Shrine with so much light, so much marble and so many bills (all of which he would pay), and still remain faithful to his confessional-box, the place of closest contact with the people of the city, where changes were taking place at top speed.

The number of inhabitants had now risen to three hundred thousand and the protagonists of the Risorgimento had by this time been transformed into equestrian or pedestrian statues in its streets and squares: Cavour, Victor Emmanuel, Lamarmora. . . And now the last of them were disappearing: General De Sonnaz who had fought in all the national wars: Louis Kossuth, the champion of Hungarian independence, who had spent his old age in Turin; the engineer Grandis, one of the drillers of the Col de Fréjus tunnel; and the great Galileo Ferraris. The autumn of 1897 saw the death of two 'standard-bearers' of Risorgimento anti-clerical journalism: G.B. Bottero, co-founder of the *Gazzetta del Popolo*, and Casimiro Teja, the extremely famous planner of the *Fischietto*. And the *Fischietto* thus died too. Meanwhile the socialist weekly *Il Grido del Popolo* began appearing in July 1892: Turin had its own Workers' Association from May 1891 and the example of Edmondo de Amicis attracted many Turinese intellectuals to the socialist movement. The appearance of Leo XIII's encyclical *Rerum Novarum* had a quite special importance for the Catholics of the city, which by this time was taking the leading part in the industrial revolution. Here, more than elsewhere, the quarrels were kindled between the adherents of the new movement known as 'Democrazia Cristiana', ready to push on beyond the limits indicated by Pope Leo, and the veterans of the *Opera dei Congressi*, very active in works but even more entrenched in their age-old intransigence.

Everyone in Turin however was concentrating on the coming Ninety-eight. For us who come afterwards, this was the year of the disturbances in Milan and General Bava-Beccaris's bombardment. But in Turin the year was busily awaited since it was a congeries of anniversaries and

71

connected demonstrations. For the State it was the fiftieth anniversary of the Statute and involved the presence of the King and Queen in the city, among other things to open a display never seen before: the first International Exhibition, accompanied by economic and literary congresses, and the homage of all the cities of Italy to Turin, the cradle of the Statute. In 1898, the secular joined with the religious for the showing of the Shroud, belonging to the House of Savoy and hence associated with dynastic occasions. For 1898, the Turinese Church on its own initiative had organized the Marian Congress and the Exhibition of Ancient and Modern Sacred Art; the fifteenth centenary of the founding of the Catholic hierarchy in Piedmont, and the fourth centenary of the cathedral also happened to fall that year.

To these religious celebrations, as to the Eucharistic congress of 1894, the new Archbishop of Turin, Davide Riccardi, devoted himself with vigorous activity; previously Bishop of Ivrea and then of Novara, he made his entry into the archdiocese on 23 March 1892. Not only that: he had completed his pastoral visitation and stirred up Catholic Action with the support of the *Opera dei Congressi*.

He had also concerned himself with the Catholic press, its problems and its quarrels. In 1893, *L'Unità Cattolica* moved to Florence; the paper had been founded by Fr Margotti after leaving *L'Armonia* (which migrated to Florence after the September Convention). The only paper left was the *Corriere Nazionale*, which was having a very hard time. The *Italia Reale* was then produced, which did no better, so it was decided to merge it with the *Corriere Nazionale*, and the paper under this double masthead was to survive until 1903. In these activities, the Archbishop made use of Giuseppe Allamano, who also became chairman of the board of *Italia Reale*, without however getting much satisfaction out of it. His preoccupation with these means of communication then prompted him to intervene when it looked as though *La Voce dell'Operaio* was on its last leg owing to the working commitments of its most popular spokesman, Domenico Giraud. Allamano came to its rescue himself, on his own authority clearing Giraud's position. The paper still appears today, under the name *Voce del Popolo*.

Thus the Archbishop called on him to serve on committees and commissions directing the major enterprises undertaken by the diocese. And they frequently met, for Archbishop Riccardi too made a habit of going to pray at the Consolata every Saturday. For the rest, Joseph Allamano by now had had plenty of experience as regards successions in the archiepiscopal palace: 'Whenever the Archbishops of Turin take possession of their see, they look at me with a certain reserve and, as it were, distrust. But later they call on my services and I have always got on extremely well with them, using all my efforts for the good of the diocese.'

With Archbishop Riccardi, however, he never addressed the matter of the missionary foundation. This absolutely tireless bishop died after ruling the diocese for barely five years; the great festivities for which he had so enthusiastically prepared were to be celebrated by another.

This other was Agostino Richelmy, dear to Leo XIII for his studies in St Thomas (but also learned in Latin, Italian literature and Mathematics). Bishop of Ivrea since 1886, on Archbishop Riccardi's death he was appointed Archbishop of Turin, taking possession on 28 November 1897.

For Joseph Allamano this time there was no initial mistrust to be overcome. With Agostino Richelmy he was on first names. They had been fellow-students, ordained in the same year. When he was a young priest in Turin, the new Archbishop had tried to keep going the 'apostolic schools' created by Canon Ortalda.

There was more still: Archbishop Richelmy, when ruling the Diocese of Ivrea, had proposed Joseph Allamano as Bishop of Saluzzo. Actually he had not been the only one to do so. His name had also been suggested by the Bishops of Fossano, Pinerolo, Cuneo and Mondovì, either as sole candidate or with others. And Archbishop Riccardi for the same post had suggested two priests from Ivrea and three from Turin, first on the list being Allamano. 'He would govern a diocese extremely well', he had written, adding however that he was not without fault. What was it? That of having wanted to be a proper canon in the Metropolitan Church of Turin; 'however, when the Chapter chose someone else, he accepted this with good grace.' Here it must be said that when Joseph Allamano actually did become a proper canon, his behaviour made it clear to everyone that he was the better canon of them all.

There were also two other curious objections advanced by Archbishop Riccardi against Allamano's being made a Bishop, in the document in which he proposed him. One was of a physical nature: 'He has the defect of having one shoulder higher than the other, which makes him look slightly humpbacked: despite this, his look is grave and dignified.' The other is really a good one: there are already such a lot of bishops who come from Castelnuovo d'Asti, 'that, if in present Piedmontese episcopal appointments it were not considered necessary to look outside Turin, it might at least seem appropriate not to take anyone from Castelnuovo d'Asti, unless one had to go back there later.'

6

Missions: We're off

In 1899, Leo XIII created Agostino Richelmy a Cardinal, as a mark of personal recognition. At the same time however this started the tradition that the Archbishop of Turin should be a cardinal. Joseph Allamano thus had a Cardinal — the first and only one — with whom to be on first names. The works at the Consolata continued and so did Giacomo Camisassa's activities with suppliers, architects and foreman. The Turinese part of the canonical investigation on Fr Giuseppe Cafasso had been completed. The next thing that had to be done was to send the findings to the Vatican. Thus it came about that the rector of the Consolata had to set out on his journeyings again. Ten years earlier, the heads of Propaganda Fide had waited for him in vain; now he is drawn to Rome by an uncle on his way to being declared a saint.

He set out in March 1899, delivered the documents and then went to the Pontifical Seminary of the Holy Apostles, a missionary institute to which, in his dream-time, he had planned to entrust the young Turinese priests whom he had trained, if. . . But none of the heads of the seminary were at home. The only person available was a Piedmontese who had just come back from China, Fr Giovanni Bonzano. To him, in a lengthy chat, Allamano unfolded his idea of training missionaries and then passing them on to an institute that would use them. Not much of a dream, said Bonzano who was seventeen years younger but an optimist in such matters: there was no point in putting oneself under someone else's authority. The Turinese canon could create his own Institute in Turin and maintain it as an independent entity, if he had the funds to do it.

As to the funds, something odd had happened already. Joseph Allamano had been named as sole beneficiary by a priest whom he barely knew, Mgr Angelo Demichelis, who had recently died. The latter bequeathed him the premises in Corso Duca di Genova of the Institute of the Annunciation for female teachers, which he had founded but which was now in decline with hardly any students; then there was a house in Rivoli and some money. More than 200,000 lire in all, when the accounts were drawn up. On the Archbishop's advice, he accepted the legacy. And a few months after his journey to Rome, he got another one. In the winter of 1899-1900, there was a serious influenza epidemic in Turin, carrying off, among others, the engineer Edoardo Felizzati who was still under fifty. He was one of his friends, a supporter of the Consolata and of various charitable causes. Allamano assisted him to the last. And then discovered that he had been left 300,000 lire.

But he too sickened of the influenza in January 1900. Perhaps he had caught it while assisting two sick people for hours in the cold; very quickly he became desperately ill. The doctors threw up their hands — double pneumonia. Giacomo Camisassa anxiously celebrated Mass in his presence; at the Pastoral Institute everyone was praying for him, and then another amazing thing happened: the Consolata filled with people. They arrived from all over Turin through the falling snow. Unbelievable: people coming in, people going out, the Shrine was constantly thronged. A measure of how much this reserved and silent canon meant to the city.

One priest had already said a Requiem Mass for him; but the sick man unexpectedly began to improve during the night of 29 January. (Later he was to recall the feast of St Francis de Sales falls on that day.) Nor was the improvement that illusory one heralding death, as one newspaper gave its readers to understand; he had really survived. And, at the prompting of the Archbishop who had hurried to his bedside, he finally ended his years of silence about the missionary plan. In his characteristic manner of speech, he was to remind anyone who indulged in talk about miracles: 'There was no question of any revelation. When I was at the point of death, I made a promise, if I was cured, to found the Institute. I was cured and the foundation was made. That's all.' Archbishop Richelmy's encouragement ('The

Institute must be founded and you are the man to do it') meant everything to him: the Archbishop's approval was the Church's consent, the voice of God. He had waited, saying nothing, for ten years rather than act without this explicit approval.

Now that he had authority on his side, he wasted no time. While still convalescing in Rivoli (in the house inherited from Mgr Demichelis) he despatched a letter to the Archbishop. This was the first step on the road to making the foundation and took place on Tuesday, 24 April 1900. At the same moment, the Duke of the Abruzzi's Arctic Expedition reached latitude 86°34'N, where no human being had ever trod, and there raised the Italian flag. For Fr Allamano however it was the feast of St Fidelis of Sigmaringen, a saint whom he had always loved. (His name was Mark Reyd: born in 1578, a law graduate of Freiburg, famous as a lawyer because he charged no fees to the poor. At the age of thirty-five, however, he became a Capuchin, taking Fidelis as his name in religion. He was killed in 1622 by Calvinist peasants, falling victim to the religious divisions between Christians, exacerbated by political rivalries.)

Let us now look at the letter that 'got the wheel going'. Joseph Allamano begins by saying that Mgr Demichelis' Annunziata Institute for school teachers now has so few pupils that a choice has to be made, whether to keep it running or to close it down. And in case of closure, 'my inclination would be to found an institute to train men for the foreign missions.' Mgr Demichelis' will, he goes on, permits this. Missionary institutes of this sort already exist in the principal cities of Italy, but not in Turin. So this is what happens: 'Various seminarians and priests will enter institutes outside Piedmont, and we have such run by the Lazarists, by the San Calogero Fathers in Milan, in Verona, in Genoa, in Piacenza and even in Algiers. But if, reluctantly, some do decide to enroll among people of different temperament, to whom they may always find themselves, as it were, playing second fiddle, many for similar reasons will abandon their vocation, while still desiring the missionary life. . .' In a word, there are young men available in Piedmont for missionary work. But they are scattered here and there or spoilt by waiting. There are even young priests leaving for the United States: 'I do not find this particularly cheering, since I fear the hope of being well paid plays a large part in it; also on account of the spiritual harm due to the isolation they will experience there, with no fatherly hand to guide them. If instead we were to train a team of Piedmontese missionaries to serve in given regions, led by their own superiors, labouring not for money but solely for love of souls, those with true vocations would be drawn in this right direction.' The letter ends as follows: 'Behold, your Eminence, how much, to the unburdening of my conscience and for the greater glory of God, I have thought fit to show you. Reflect on the matter before the Lord, and on my early return to Turin I hope you will give me the word go.'

Cardinal Agostino Richelmy gave him the word go in a conversation, the concluding words of which were to be imprinted in the memory of all the Consolata missionaries: 'In your letter you said more against than in favour of the foundation. Nevertheless you must make it, because it is God's will.' To which Allamano replied: 'Very well, your Eminence, in your name I shall pay out the nets!'

To Rome, to Rome

A request was sent off to Propaganda Fide in June. Allamano explained that he now had the full consent of his Bishop and that, this being so, the Missionary Institute would now come into proper existence. He did however need the Roman Congregation to assign him the territory in which the future evangelizers were to work. That is to say, 'that part of Equatorial East Africa which is bounded to the south by the left bank of the River Tana and northern slopes of Mount Kenya; to the west by a line which, passing through Lakes Baringo and Norok (Rudolf), continues to the sources of the River Omo; to the north by the headwaters of the Omo and Juba; to the east by the right bank of the River Webi Shebeli down to the Benadir coast, under Italian protectorate.'

The request was detailed since Allamano (and Giacomo Camisassa too) wanted right-away to have a definite field of work, so as to permit a targeted preparation for the candidates, and which at the same time could be clearly identified to the faithful, so they would know where their contributions were to be spent. But Propaganda Fide thought otherwise: all African territory had already been parcelled up into Vicariates Apostolic (some of them very extensive and with very few missionaries); there were no 'virgin' lands left, to hand out to institutes in the making. For this reason, the procedure to be followed was this: Allamano should apply to the Vicar Apostolic responsible for the territory to which he wanted to send his missionaries; there they would serve their apprenticeship, after which it would be easy enough for them to exercise their ministry 'under their own roof'.

Fr Camisassa then set out for Rome, armed also with a note from Cardinal Richelmy. He talked, he negotiated, he discussed and reported back to Turin that agreement would have to be reached with the Vicar Apostolic of the Galla, while the Institute was being created in Turin with the Archbishop's consent. Further, he added: better still if the other bishops of Piedmont give their approval as well. The letter ended on a rudely concrete note as regards the Prefect of Propaganda Fide: 'This evening I am wondering whether I should call on Cardinal Ledòkowski again, but they tell me he is in a state where he does *nothing* and is *more dead than alive*, so that any answer he might give me would be worthless, that is to say, no force could be attached to it since he is no longer the effective head of Propaganda Fide.'

The letter arrived, as it happened, just before all the bishops of Piedmont were holding a meeting in Turin, at the Consolata. Cardinal Richelmy expounded and warmly recommended the missionary project to them and all approved it. On 29 January 1901, the feast of St Francis de Sales, an archiepiscopal decree made Joseph Allamano's dream come true: '. . . We cordially approve this new work to be known as the Consolata Institute for Foreign Missions (*Istituto della Consolata per le Missioni Estere*).'

Superior of the Institute: Joseph Allamano. Headquarters: the house formerly belonging to Mgr Demichelis in Corso Duca di Genova, where on 18 July 1901, the altar was consecrated in the chapel, which already existed but had now been enlarged so as to serve the people of the neighbourhood as well. The first little group of candidates for the missions started living and studying in the building, which soon acquired the nickname of 'Consolatina' (Little Consolata). A teacher of English volunteered his services at once: this was Fr Giovanni Battista Balangero of Envie, Cuneo, who had been a missionary in Australia and then in Ceylon (now Sri Lanka). A rule of life was observed, which Allamano had prepared some time before, and his advice was followed as occasion arose: short notes from the Consolata, suggestions and advice in his soft voice.

But other voices were singing a different song among the Turinese clergy. To many of them, this seemed pure folly: Allamano already had his hands full with that work at the Consolata, all those expensive slabs of marble arriving in convoy by the cartload, paintings, new altars. . . and away he goes, involving himself in some missionary nonsense of sending people to Africa at his own expense. 'He'll end up like Ortalda' was the prophecy current among the more sceptical of the clergy. And one of Allamano's priests used to go out of his way in the street so as not to have to meet any of his colleagues, knowing at least one out of two would say something nasty about the Institute and its lunatic of a superior. Even Bishop Bertagna, Allamano's fellow-townsman, went about spreading pessimism. He even went and said dismal things to the excellent Fr Nicolis di Robilant, though here he miscalculated sadly. Fr Nicolis was so disgusted by this disloyalty, he decided to counter it with deeds: and big deeds too. We anticipate events a little but it seems right to say it straightaway. Dismayed at what Bishop Bertagna had said, Fr Nicolis went home and decided to make his will, bequeathing a robust legacy to the canon: two dairy farms at Verolengo, his books and the gold chalice presented to him for his First Mass.

In February 1904 Fr Nicolis died, leaving Fr Cafasso's biography unfinished. Allamano, who had assisted him on his deathbed, only learnt what he had inherited once the will was read. And he immediately made up his mind to refuse: 'For it is a maxim with me that the Institute needs esteem, a good name, more than money. . . What did I do? I said: "I accept the chalice, I accept the library, but I can't accept the two dairy farms." ' The difficulty was settled then, largely thanks to the mother of the deceased, by a donation: one of the brothers bought the dairy farms, paying the purchase price to the rector of the Consolata; and the latter accepted the money but insisted on pledging himself to pay over the annual interest on it to a Di Robilant who had fallen on hard times.

'Esteem, good name. . .' This was one of the hinges of Allamano's life and one of the characteristics of his works. Whether concerning the Shrine or missionary expeditions, he always sought for support among the ordinary people of Turin. His ambition was to deserve the support of those very many who could only give a few lira, since this meant rooting initiatives and undertakings in the popular mind, calling on everyone to play a part; while at the same time remaining free of patronage and protectorates. It meant, in brief, living in the present; perhaps even a little in advance of it. Certainly the reserved Canon Allamano did not join the Catholic vanguard, that source of alarm to the hierarchy; for instance, the Christian Democrats who, in Turin especially, were an attractive and combative presence (or an extremely inconvenient one, depending on the way you looked at them). But he kept in step with the times and changes, thanks to the link that he maintained in person with every class in the city, every hour of the day; including those spent in the confessional which put him in touch with the good and the bad among the Turinese, in this period of continuous change, virtually a change a day. Few people in July 1899 knew that a car factory called Fiat had been founded but in the following March these initials appeared over a workshop in Corso Dante. Transport in the city was largely by trams, belonging to the Società Belga-Torinese, but cars had already appeared in the streets and the Municipal Council was obliged to set the first speed limits for them: not faster than a trotting horse. The world of labour saw the first trade strikes: heavy industry, gas, and a first attempt at a general strike in solidarity with the gas workers. In the early days of 1902, Turin was to be linked by telephone line to Paris; Via Arsenale and Via Santa Teresa began filling up with large banks.

Corso Duca di Genova harboured the dreams of the first

little missionary group — and the founder's. The latter was certainly not indifferent to the critical voices, sometimes authoritative; it can also be assumed that he used to wonder whether the undertaking was not rather late in the day. At the seminary, at the Pastoral Institute and at the Consolata, he had always been exceptionally prompt in discharging his responsibilities, in dealing with important assignments. In missionary work however, he was making his debut when over fifty, he being the same age as the Archbishop. The great figures of the Turinese Church had all gone: Don Bosco, the volcanic Fr Cocchi of the first oratories and of the Artigianelli, Fr Murialdo, and first and foremost those great spiritual directors, Felice Carpignano and Marcantonio Durando, both of whom he would often go and consult. And Fr di Robilant with whom he had so often talked about Fr Cafasso. All disappeared — leaving him examples, memories, even legacies — who for him had been saints walking the streets of Turin.

Now it happened that young men would talk to him in his turn and afterwards murmur: 'He must be a saint.' Now it was his generation manning the front line in the Church of Turin. There he was, at a still vigorous and creative age, but already more susceptible to fits of pessimism; a little more in need of approval than he would have been at thirty. Good must be done well, he would say. Yet there was also a need to get things done quickly. To dispel doubts and stimulate support for the new work, there was a need for people to see the new missionaries leaving as soon as possible. But to this, the *Imitation* replied: 'You are none the holier for being praised, and none the worse for being blamed. You remain what you are, nor can you be accounted greater than you are in the sight of God. If you take heed to what you are inwardly, you will not mind what men say about you' (II, 6, 2).

Foothold in Africa

There were eleven aspirant missionaries at the Consolatina, some priests, some brothers. They were being prepared on the one hand with a deepening of their spiritual life, and on the other with an intensive practical apprenticeship. Besides studying English, there were lessons in general medicine with special reference to illnesses typical to Africa and to oculistics, and practical nursing at the Ospedale di San Giovanni. Other subjects for study were: mathematics, natural sciences, rudiments of law. Lastly, they learned how to ride in the meadows of the Martinetto, and carpentry taught by Signor Caneparo, whom they all remembered afterwards for his skill and his strictness.

Meanwhile an unexpected problem had arisen: where were they to go? As early as 1891, Allamano had pin-pointed the place to which he wanted to send his missionaries: among Guglielmo Massaia's Galla — the work of one Piedmontese carried on by other Piedmontese. It not being possible to go to the Galla in Ethiopia, he had turned his eyes southwards to the Galla lands under British and, partly, Italian control (the zone 'of the ports' or Benadir, which for a while was to form part of the Italian colony of Somalia). And now he had applied to Bishop André Jarosseau, a French Capuchin who, as Vicar Apostolic, supervised missionary activity throughout the Galla lands. The latter immediately agreed to the coming, on a trial basis, of missionaries from the Turinese Institute, who would therefore work under his jurisdiction. He also indicated the area — near Lake Rudolf — where they could settle.

A fine idea, but impractical. For it turned out that neither the British nor the Italian authorities would allow Europeans into that region, since there was absolutely no way of guaranteeing their safety. On this occasion the Consolata missionaries first made the acquaintance of Giulio Pestalozza, then Italian Consul in Zanzibar: a splendid figure of a servant of his country in those very difficult places and situations, and an enlightened Christian. He was to have his place in the missionary story now beginning.

Acting on his advice, Canon Allamano next made contact with another missionary from France: Bishop Emile Allgeyer of the Congregation of the Holy Ghost, Vicar Apostolic in the territory of Southern Zanguebar, Kenya. As it happens, he just needed people — subordinates — since the British authorities had suggested he should found a mission in the green territory inhabited by the Kikuyu near

Mount Kenya, over whom reigned Chief Karoli of the thirty-nine wives. By all means let the Piedmontese come, although they were barely apprentices. Agreement was reached through negotiations which also involved the head of the Holy Ghost Fathers in Paris.

The whole episode is told in few words, but it took months of study, of meetings, a massive correspondence with Rome, Africa, Paris, consultation with governments of London and Rome. An activity that would have been impossible for Allamano with all his other responsibilities, had he not had Giacomo Camisassa at his side. He too a canon now, for since the days of Archbishop Riccardi he had been a member of the Cathedral Chapter, first in an honorary and later in an effective capacity. This theologian from Caramagna Piemonte who had held chairs of Moral Theology and Law, was a man of study and prayer, but also of practical affairs. We have already seen, and we still see, him supervising the work at the Consolata; on occasion his arrival unleashes panic. Now, with the missionary enterprise, Allamano had him permanently at hand when plans were being made and then when they were carried out. Together they studied the problems and difficulties, then Camisassa would leave, to go and speak, or write, negotiate, question religious communities, government departments, the Holy See.

He was thrilled by the preparatory work for the expedition. Doing good well, in Allamano's phrase, meant in this case missionaries equipped to the limits of the foreseeable and therefore near to self-sufficiency, without having to dissipate their energies in all directions. So the portable altar needed to be special and Camisassa invented one for the missionaries: light but robust. They were even provided with plenty of ink and pen-nibs. And, in addition, a camera: slides of Africa would be of extraordinary importance in the hands of those drumming up support for the missions.

There was one problem however. Bishop Allgeyer would accept missionaries, yes, but he did not want too many of them. Actually, they will be only four: two priests Tommaso Gays and Filippo Perlo, and two brothers Celeste Lusso and Luigi Falda. This meant that seven had to stay on at Corso Duca di Genova. A big disappointment, with worse to come.

Now came the moment for the first departure. On 3 May,

they were given their crucifixes in the little Church of the Consolatina. On 7 May, those who were leaving went to the archbishop's palace to take their leave of Cardinal Richelmy; he arranges to be left alone with them, makes them sit side by side and then kneels down to kiss their feet, and commands not to speak of the matter for a year. At last, on 8 May 1902, they set off by train from Porta Nuova Station with Joseph Allamano's final blessing. Fr Camisassa accompanies them as far as Marseilles, where they board the German vessel *Oxus* on 10 May. And on 28 May, they disembarked at Zanzibar where Consul Giulio Pestalozza was waiting for them. His help simplified things and his cordiality enspirited; the missionaries wrote about him to Allamano, who immediately sent him a letter of thanks: 'My prayers for my missionaries by now can no longer be distinguished from those for Your Lordship and family. . .' He was to try and get him awarded a decoration by Giulio Prinetti, foreign minister in the Zanardelli government. But without success.

The expedition had Fr Gays as its superior and Fr Perlo, Canon Camisassa's nephew as bursar, formerly bursar of the Shrine in Turin. Now he was also to be the correspondent for the bulletin *La Consolata* with accounts of life in Africa, which increased its popularity and circulation. It was he who described the unexpected meeting with Chief Karoli, who welcomed the little group very warmly at Nairobi.

On the evening of 28 June, after a train journey and then one in caravan with porters, they arrived at the place designated for the mission to the Kikuyu: Tuthu, two thousand metres above sea level and two days' march from Mount Kenya. Next day, the feast of Sts Peter and Paul, Mass was celebrated for the first time on Kikuyu soil. The Kikuyu population watched the newcomers and how they settled in. There was interest, friendly curiosity. Problems were to arise shortly, but these came from the whites.

There was a visit from an official of the British administration at Tuthu, followed by an astounding report to the Government Commissioner, full of wild accusations against the missionaries and recommending they should be quickly thrown out. Indeed, the order to leave arrived; and the four Piedmontese, in agreement with Bishop Allgeyer, decided to stay where they were. There had to be something behind it: distrust of Catholic missionaries, problems with the local population, and indeed the problem of their safety raised its head once more. Perhaps one of the reasons was the absence of the British assistant commissioner, Stanley Hinde, who was a friend of the Kikuyus and of missionaries of all denominations. The four men from Turin meanwhile very calmly discussed and studied possible solutions. No blows were struck, there was nothing to frighten them. The natives continued to treat them pleasantly, hundreds of people attended the clinic the moment it was set up. The incident dragged on for a while and ended in a way that favoured a plan of the missionaries: that of creating a sort of base camp (they called it a mission procure) somewhere quickly accessible from the coast. This place was to be Limuru, on the railway from Mombasa to Lake Victoria.

In Turin: everyone gone

The crisis averted in Africa burst in Turin instead. Seven men stayed in the Institute in Corso Duca di Genova after the expedition left. Now everyone had gone away. For a long while, a dramatized version of what happened would be told: Canon Allamano, all unsuspecting, arrives at the Consolatina and finds it deserted, abandoned by all; so he locks up, puts the key in his pocket and goes back to the Shrine, where he says to the Consolata (Our Lady of Consolation): 'I've done my best. It's your problem now!'

Things did not occur literally like that. Even so, that was the substance of it. After the four had departed, the other seven went away: all of them, even if not all at once nor in such a way as to leave the house empty. Disappointment, resentment at not having gone, lack of confidence in the future or the finding of other channels for their individual vocations: many factors undoubtedly played a part, and in any case Allamano let them go, respecting their right to choose.

It was a very heavy blow however. There was a barrage of 'I told you so!' and reminders of 'How Ortalda ended up' with his own missionary institutes. And besides, what could any parish priest in Turin or out in the country say, with the best will in the world, to a lad who might go to him for advice about the Institute? 'Humph, the whole lot of them left. . .'

Without raising his voice, without lessening his good manners, Joseph Allamano stood firm under the storm. Yes, those lads had gone away, but others were coming. There had indeed been mistakes, but these would be put right. For instance, the Institute had not had a director; giving one of the priests the role of *primus inter pares* (first among equals) had caused dissension rather than good-feeling. So he appointed a director from outside: the junior curate of San Gioacchino, Fr Luigi Borio. New candidates started arriving: twenty enrolled in December 1902, of whom two were priests, fourteen were seminarians (of these, seven coming from the Cottolengo, the Thomasites), and four laymen. The two priests were Antonio Borda Bossano and Gabriele Perlo, Filippo's brother. (A third Perlo brother was to enter in 1903.)

From the start, a few sisters had been attached to the staff of the Consolatina: two or three, depending on circumstances. They belonged to the Poor Daughters of San Gaetano, a small and valuable congregation founded at Pancalieri by the parish priest, Fr Giovanni Maria Boccardo during the cholera of 1884 to help poor people left without support.

With the new arrivals, new expeditions could be considered. The reports from Africa with their informed comments about the equipment were of great help in working out an even better balance in what was to be sent. Here, Canon Camisassa lived his finest hours (at night would often wake up with some new idea which he would instantly jot down in a notebook lying to hand). The scheme was to build a sawmill in the forest and a joiner's shop, using water as source of energy by means of a recent American invention, the Pelton hydraulic turbine. The canon would go and negotiate, discuss, contrive with the engineers in Turinese factories. Giuseppe and Gian Paola Mina were to write: 'A large band-saw, mechanical planes, morticer, drill, Pelton turbine, all were made "to measure" in the sense of being made in sections, so that they could be taken to pieces of a size a man could carry on his shoulder, once they arrived at the railhead.' So Giacomo Camisassa was a special client for these firms and to a certain degree a collaborator: 'As a mechanic, Camisassa tackled the problems, made inventive decisions, dealt with the foundry, made sure everything was solidly packed and could stand up to being off-loaded at ports where there were no cranes. He put forward designs, sections, lucid plans with minute descriptions, right down to the last bolt. . . In the course of years, he was by the same methods to make various machines for processing coffee: mills.'

Little by little what was getting ready in Turin was no longer or not only what the missionaries needed for themselves and for helping others, as for instance the medical supplies. It gradually became something more, which would be of direct use to the people of Kenya as an instrument of cultural promotion. For instance, when a complete printing-press arrived from Turin, it was used to print the *Wathiomo Mokinyu* (*The True Friend*), Kenya's first monthly newspaper.

The second expedition (four missionaries) set off in December 1902. And for the next one, planned for spring 1903, there was to be an unexpected novelty: along with the six missionaries were to go eight sisters too: the first women called to the work of the Consolata Missions.

It was an unexpected novelty for the outside observer. As a matter of fact, sisters had been considered very early on, taking into account how much many female congregations had been contributing for so long. Already, on the eve of the first expedition, Allamano had informed Consul Pestalozza, via Camisassa, that there would have to be a mission procure somewhere along the railway, since, among other reasons, 'in time and not so far off either, we may send out some nuns, under our people's authority, to attend to all the linen needed by the missionaries inland, run the schools, etc.'

And Fr Filippo Perlo, having barely arrived in Africa, was to turn this forecast into a request, stressing very optimistically in his letters what grand prospects were opening up for evangelization. This was what he wrote to Camisassa as early as July 1902 in his anxiety — one might almost say frenzy — to get going: 'For now, tell the rector: if he cares to send 100–200 missionaries, he only has to take his pick. At every step there are splendid peoples to evangelize. . . In principle, if the missionaries are untrained, let him send them like that; if they cannot speak any languages, never mind; here they will learn all that is needed, by talking to the natives and getting themselves known. For the main thing now is to occupy the best positions. . . Because of this, if there are not many priests, let him send sisters. We shall convert the Kikuyu with the sisters. They will run schools for the little boys and girls; they will tend the sick and, what is more important still, they will relieve the missionaries of a thousand petty matters that prevent them from attending to their ministry and reduce them to some degree in the estimation of the natives.'

An institute of female missionaries is certainly not thinkable as yet, and Allamano has in fact to look for sisters who are already professed elsewhere. Canon Giuseppe Ferrero, of the Little House of Divine Providence and fourth successor to Fr Cottolengo, helped him by making a group of Vincentian Sisters available.

There were to be eight of these in the first group, leaving in April 1903 with five priests and a lay brother. Fr Perlo had insisted on this from Africa, and Allamano in Turin had had problems in constructing and equipping the expedition. But no time was lost. And so the sisters disembarked in Africa almost before they were expected and for a time were obliged to stop in Limuru. Eventually, on 23 July, they reached Morang'a where a stone house had been built for them at top speed. With them, they had brought a series of recommendations from Joseph Allamano, via Camisassa, for Fr Perlo: 'The rector wishes everyone to take a glass of wine with their meals, especially the sisters.' Here we have a sort of echo of the Apostle Paul's recommendation to Timothy ('No longer drink only water, but use a little wine. . .'). But it also shows an affectionate preoccupation with them all, especially after certain complaints reaching Turin from Africa: Fr Perlo is too strict, first of all with himself, but also with everyone else. With the energies that missionaries need, so much severity becomes a danger, and the rector invites Fr Perlo — in another of his Piedmontese metaphors — to 'widen his hand' or, in other words, to let everybody have a bit more food.

7

Africa and the spirits

There was no talking during meals; they listened to readings. In those days this was the common rule in religious orders as in seminaries, and so it was in Turin in the Pastoral Institute as in the Consolata Missionary Institute. All sorts of things were read: passages from the Bible, pages from the Fathers of the Church, lives of the saints, annals of the missions. Joseph Allamano added another topic: the norms of good manners, the book of etiquette. We do not know which particular text he used (at the time, the Abbé Branchereau's treatise *On Ecclesiastical Courtesies and Good Manners* was the best known), but the substance is what counts. He did not confine himself to suggesting what gestures to perform and what to omit; he insisted above all that relations with others must in their original inspiration be based on charity. Once this is grasped, good behaviour flows from it more or less automatically.

At the school of Joseph Allamano, in brief, they also learned good taste: which he had always had, being born with it and which he radiated on those about him. Here is one of his sayings: 'Being coarse means being on the verge of something worse.' And round him he succeeded in establishing a peculiar climate of always deferential familiarity, such as also made itself felt round the great Cardinal Andrea Ferrari, Archbisbop of Milan. 'When you were with him,' remarked a canon who had been his colleague, 'you were naturally brought to seriousness and restraint.'

And now this teaching had a specific application for the missionaries: 'Let no one say: we only have to go to Africa and be with the savages. What! Are negroes not human beings like us? Below the surface of a black skin, they have a kind heart and sensitive feelings. And besides, who ever said that Our Lord spoke or behaved coarsely, just because he had to live with the apostles, who were rough? Did he not rather attract them to himself by his pleasing manners? In this too, you are and should appear to be true representatives of Jesus.'

Bad news from Africa, meanwhile. Fr Tommaso Gays, as we have said, had been appointed superior of the mission, with Fr Filippo Perlo as bursar. But the situation was an unrealistic one, especially with the new arrivals and the expansion of the mission's activities. Filippo Perlo continued to treat Tommaso Gays as 'very dear superior' but in fact did everything himself, or almost so. In a word, he was the head, and so everyone else considered him. Also because in those early days, there was not always a very clear distinction between what pertained to the spiritual (for which the superior was responsible) and those temporal, practical, administrative problems which a bursar is appointed precisely to deal with. Here, within the limits of his responsibilities, and also beyond them, Filippo Perlo was the one who gave the orders, while Tommaso Gays apparently assented to it all. There was no antagonism between the two: he who was superior only in name was the first to acknowledge the effective superior's qualities and admire them. . . In the end, he decided to send in his resignation to Turin, with the proposal that Filippo Perlo be given the title of superior. In doing so, Gays used a method he was later to describe as 'fraudulent', that is to say, he gave Allamano to believe that the whole mission already knew about his resignation, proffered and accepted, while it was no such thing.

Distance too perhaps favoured misunderstandings. The fact remains that between the end of 1903 and the beginning of 1904, the situation was regularized, with Filippo Perlo appointed as the superior. And Allamano did not appoint any more bursars, leaving it to whoever was in charge there to find himself such helpers as occasion required.

Even so, that was not the worst news. During October and November 1903, almost all the sisters who had arrived that spring fell ill; there was talk of typhus, of other diseases, mainly of malaria. And two of them died during that period: Sr Editta Vivori and Sr Giordana Sopegno. Two others had to be repatriated. The group of nuns was reduced by half.

Faced with this crisis, Allamano thought it urgent to show

92

firmness, to keep everyone's spirits up. So he ratified the departure of a new expedition. On 12 January 1904, another twelve Cottolengo sisters arrived in Africa with five missionaries. At that point there were sixteen sisters in the field, working in the Consolata Missions but belonging to another congregation with other superiors. An important example of collaboration, and also of difficulties and embarrassments, with the priests and laymen owing obedience to Allamano, and the sisters owing it to the superior of the Little House; with, before them, the extremely tough task of making a first contact with peoples whose language they did not know, of travelling through village after village treating the sick, getting to know families, making the first attempts to open schools.

Like the male missionaries, they periodically sent their diaries to Allamano. And this allowed him to keep constantly abreast not only of their problems, but more important still — given his care about individuals — of each one's state of mind.

Here is a description from Sr Gundene Endrizzi's diary of the life led by the nuns in those early days: 'Today we treated more than a hundred sick people. Each day there are more of them; there are always new ones, with sores that would make you shudder.' 'After midday, the Assistant Mother and Sr Angela go into the villages; they visit about twenty of them. . .' And here is how one of their initial tasks, that of being assigned to household duties, was gradually replaced by front-line responsibilities: 'Sr Angela, from now on, will spend as little time in the kitchen as possible, Fr Gabriele having put in three boys who will prepare the food for them. He has done this so that the sisters can be freer, two of them to go every day into the villages and the other two to give medical treatment at home.' 'In the evening we go to bed really late, because we eat late and then there are those blessed — not to say worse — jiggers which cause us to waste a lot of time.' In Sr Agnesina's diary, there is the recurrent theme of being hungry: 'We sit down to dinner, all with a tremendous appetite; we could even eat the table legs. And this appetite is with us nearly every day.' 'We get home all with a big appetite. It's a pity when the appetite comes on outside meal-times, for since there is no bread here there is absolutely nothing to stay its pangs.'

The Vicar Apostolic, Bishop Allgeyer, became a great admirer of the sisters and wrote to Joseph Allamano about them: 'The Little House sisters have edified me everywhere. Without fear of being mistaken, I can say that they are full of apostolic spirit; they are like angels in the midst of the blacks and without any doubt are the admiration of human beings, of angels and of God.'

In the first days of March 1904, a gathering of all the missionary priests was held at Morang'a (its English name being Fort Hall) for a retreat, followed by a series of meetings for an exchange of first experiences and in the light of these for drawing up a work plan, 'so as to be able to proceed in the common work with unity of intention and action', as Allamano was to write in his report for Propaganda Fide in April 1905. This meeting and the ones that at intervals were to follow it came to be known in the history of the Consolata Missions as the 'Morang'a Conferences'.

In all, there were ten participants at the first conference; plus two more in Turin: Joseph Allamano and Giacomo Camisassa, who spent endless hours poring over reports, diaries, letters, and who immersed themselves in the reality of the Kikuyu from the rooms of the Consolata. Joseph Allamano, who had trained so many priests without ever having been a junior curate, was now called to this other undertaking: of guiding missionaries in a country they were seeing for the first time and he had never seen and never would.

But his was no inspired improvization, no gift of nature. At least, not only that. As a basis, there was always his accurate analysis of problems, there were his everlasting notes, there was a history of evangelization exhaustively investigated. In this examination too, Joseph Allamano had prepared his texts well.

So far, no news of conversions, of baptisms, had arrived from the land of the Kikuyu. Instead there were all the problems of getting established and the struggle to achieve self-sufficiency: to intercept the water for the Pelton turbine, to canalize it, to find out how to obtain energy from it and get the sawmill working in the forest, and then the joiner's shop. This was the most pressing and important work, since with the wood huts and furniture could be made. And already, even if in very miniature form, this work, into which the missionary priests and brothers had flung themselves, began attracting the notice of the blacks and the participation of one or two: the first absolutely unprepared apprentices, who had nonetheless already taken a step of gigantic importance. By working and then by involving at least one or two of the natives in the work, the missionary achieved his first and essential aim: that of establishing a distinction between himself and the other whites, whom the blacks regarded as bringing bad luck more than anything else.

Before all else it was essential to make the people understand that 'Father (the missionary) is not the Governor.' From the diary of Gabriele Perlo (Filippo's brother) in October 1903 we read: 'We are going to Morang'a. . . in the Ngiombe district. The population, having only a few months ago received a fearful shaking from the Governor, will be timid to begin with. . .' The Governor's arrival meant forced collections of tribute, extortions practised by the soldiery from hut to hut, then the customary brutality towards the women. The missionary's arrival, in contrast, meant cordiality and help, interest in community and individual, respect for their customs.

Allamano had warned the missionaries right from the start: no one at the Consolata was expecting quick and sensational results. And they too must avoid this temptation, '. . . and with patience the day of harvest will come. By people who do not understand, you will be asked if you are baptizing yet; they do not realize that your work is preparing the mass conversion of that people; and that the important thing is not to spend time in one particular activity and place to the prejudice of the majority.' From the Morang'a Conference, the missionaries echo his approach: 'Given the character and customs of the Akikuyu, it looks as if the best means of starting our relationship with them can be reduced to the following: catechism classes, schools, village visits, mission clinics, environmental training.'

Initially it was a matter, not so much of talking about God *to* these people, as of talking about him *with* them. And of thus gradually coming to know — here the language problems were a really serious obstacle — how they thought of God. And of drafting the very first catechisms, brief texts which in very simple terms would give a picture of God as

95

absolute righteousness, of human beings as endowed with immortal souls, of the devil not as a sort of 'equal' to God but forever subject to him. . .

This religious instruction could be given more or less anywhere, even in the forest, half an hour's conversation in the morning before starting work, or in the mission stations, or in the villages. The population had their own idea of God as 'essentially good' and of a demon to whom everything bad was due: 'We are therefore into Christian theology, even if it is incomplete', Filippo Perlo noted in his diary. 'Sacrifices to the devil, rather than being a true sacrifice, are the equivalent of throwing a dog a bone so that he won't bite you.' There are the *ngoma*, say the Kikuyu, and to these bad spirits which can inflict serious harm, one has to make offerings and sacrifices, so that they will leave people alone. For the Christian and for the Christian missionary, there is a strong temptation to attack this belief head-on, as a superstition to be routed. This attitude of mind is common in the diaries. In Turin, Allamano reads them and immediately intervenes with a message to Perlo, the superior, who was in turn to pass it on to everybody: 'It is of the greatest importance, especially when visiting the villages, not to speak openly against the superstitions, sacrifices and *ngoma* of the Akikuyu, however idolatrous and immoral they may be. This is a matter requiring the greatest prudence; they are practices that will later collapse of their own accord. At present it is better to pretend not to notice them.' And, he goes on, transcribing the message Rector Allamano has sent from Turin for everybody's attention: 'I see from the diaries that some of you are inveighing against the *ngoma*. For heaven's sake go gently, as we do here about dances, even though the *ngoma* are worse. We have to dissimulate the evil, since it is impossible now to overcome this difficulty, and fighting it head-on would be prejudicial to conversions. I was reading a few days ago how conversions were proceeding at a great rate in China all the while Fr Ricci, the Jesuit, permitted certain offerings to the dead. . . Some narrow-minded people opposed this, and this in turn provoked persecution and the end of good results. In removing the evil, you will need time and patience.'

96

In a word, conversion was not to aim at individuals but at the masses. And it was not to be the point of departure for some unknown adventure; it was to be the point of arrival, the harmonious conclusion of a work of a total raising of this people, beginning from their culture of the day, not by sweeping it away but by giving it a directed development. Then every baptism, rather than being a 'victory for the missionary', will be the sanction of a common conquest, of the one who has set forth the faith and the one who has accepted it. If at the end of the twentieth century there are vigorous local Churches with their own pastors, flourishing in this territory, the reason why is hidden in the years of sowing at the beginning of the century, in the joint work of the missionaries on site and the rector piloting them from Turin, in the shadow of the Consolata.

The 'new' Consolata

'The very organizers of the procession had certainly not foreseen that the event would take on such extraordinarily grandiose proportions, for had they foreseen this they would certainly have taken measures to see that the function had taken place more quickly and ended earlier in the evening. Certainly the result was an imposing religious display, which has no precedent in the memory of middle-aged Turinese. . . What more can be said about the extraordinary crowd that for five or six hours was held captive in the streets to witness the passing of the procession?' Thus said the daily paper *La Stampa* of 20 June 1904, that is the day after the procession round the Shrine a-glitter with lights and marble, which had gone on for five hours. The completion of the long-lasting works was feted on the eight hundredth anniversary of the discovery of the picture. A very rare event as regards grandeur and the number of people taking part, helped also by a slight change in atmosphere. *La Stampa* spoke fairly favourably of the event, the paper regarded as being nearest to Giovanni Giolitti, who was the occupant of Palazzo Braschi in Rome as Prime Minister and Minister of the Interior. It was the beginning of what was to be remembered, and also regretted, as the 'Giolitti decade', having its lights and shades certainly, but also having definite conviction. This big man of the old Kingdom of Sardinia was not absolutely terrified of the entry of the Catholic and socialist masses into public life, as his predecessors had been. Furthermore, he did not frequent the Lodges, so no Masonic Grand-master was in a position to send him threatening telegrams, as he used to do to Francesco Crispi. And consistent with this, he made his officials work in the provinces, and these became legendary as 'Giolitti's prefects', 'Giolitti's police chiefs': men who had learnt not to lose their heads over a strike and not to back down at the first fuss they had over processions. So, also from the point of view of public order, the procession and all the festivities in general for the Consolata's eighth centenary took place without hitch. One single incident: a fainting fit for Cardinal Callegari, Bishop of Padua, brought on by the huge throng.

There were other Cardinals present too: Andrea Ferrari of Milan, Domenico Svampa of Bologna, and Vincenzo Vannutelli, Archbishop of the Roman Basilica of Saint Mary Major. Allamano had done things well in advance, by also inviting the Patriarch of Venice, Cardinal Giuseppe Sarto; but in the July of 1903 Pope Leo XIII died, Cardinal Sarto was elected to his place with the name Pius X, and at this period the Roman pontiffs never set foot outside the Vatican.

In the solemnity of the rites, among the hues of Cardinals and Bishops, you had to be shrewd to discover the architect of what was taking place. Not all knew Joseph Allamano by sight, not all could identify him, a silent, recollected figure who tended to be found in the second or third row during the ceremonies. Yet this could have been a day of revenge for all those years — five, ten, even more — of backbiting over his plan for the Shrine, over the outlay 'which he will never manage to pay off'. And he, year after year, had never reacted, constraining himself to an heroic patience, 'ruminating' over pages in the *Imitation of Christ* to find the foundations of true peace and the guide to forbearance. As Fr Sales was to testify: 'It is truly admirable that he could have so succeeded in this struggle against himself, with an exemplary self-mastery in words and deeds. That he had to struggle was quite clear. Sometimes one could see him go rigid with the effort to maintain his self-control; at other times he blushed, but still he kept control of himself.'

Not to mention the other volley of accusations: those about the Missionary Institute; he heard himself pointed out as the man who would ruin the diocese by robbing it of its priests on the one hand, and of contributions on the other; as the adventurer who sent men and women to defeat in Africa, without having the backing of an established congregation with resources, traditions, experience; without any backing other than Giacomo Camisassa, and so doomed to see the whole thing collapse very soon, after the initial 'flash in the pan'. And not reply, and put up with it, and let them talk, and write. . . This man, who holds his tongue and stands aloof in the splendid Shrine, could now reply, before cardinals and bishops, with a very solemn homily which probably it was his right to give: for was he not the rector of the Shrine and the Missions?

Joseph Allamano did not speak. Out of an heroic capacity for forbearance. And out of good taste. For everything spoke for him. And above all, the thronging crowds of the great festal days and then of the subsequent weeks. The crowd it was that had helped him to renovate the Consolata by paying absolutely all the bills. Above all, it was the crowd that he, Canon Joseph Allamano, had known how to put into a state of mission. It was the Turinese Church that, thanks to him, discovered the call to evangelize and gave him powerful assistance for Africa. In the summer of 1904 he was already at work on bringing the missionary settlement to independence: something which, among others, was also to involve the earmarking of regular contributions either from the Work for the Propagation of the Faith or from the Holy See. It could not be mentioned openly yet, but this was the plan; and for the time being, each despatch of people and material to Africa depended mainly on personal faith in Joseph Allamano throughout Piedmont and particularly in Turin, which had now recovered its fighting spirit.

In the spring of 1904, the first 'International Motor Show' was held at the Valentino Park, an audacious preface to future shows of the sort. The moment of the four-wheeler had come. The first Automobile Club had come into existence in Turin a few years earlier, to be followed by those of Brescia and Rome, with barons and counts at their head. The car, it was said, was taking the place of the horse, in its social implications too. But that was not the whole of it. A machine actually has to be made; technicians, skilled workmen, mechanics, test-drivers are needed. And so, round the automobile and its clubs there gathered a complete world of craftsmen who had come from the workshop and the forge: a virtually inter-class solidarity between marquis and mechanic, and the mechanic might also become a famous racing-driver or designer: two goals awaiting the Valsesian Vincenzo Lancia, for example, who now makes his debut as special driver for ministers and celebrities being driven round Turin in Fiat motors. Buying car shares briefly became a national fever, at least among those who had the means. Luigi Einaudi was to recall: 'Ignorant savers led to the slaughter in the anterooms of the stock exchanges, the frenetic world of the astute promoter, the manufacturer of joint stock company shares who had yet to buy the land on which his establishment was to be built. . . run by engineers who were still students in the classroom. . .'

But in Turin, not so. In Turin, things were done properly. 'The impression made on them by the work, the feverish movement of the machines, makes them hold work in honour and awakens the urge to imitate, to learn so as to improve their living conditions. . . The lasting effects of this are shown by those who are anxious for the things that civilization brings. . .' This, for instance, was a letter written in Turin. And it might well have been signed by some keen pioneer of industry. In fact, it was signed by Giacomo Camisassa, and its recipient was a brother in the African missions, Benedetto Falda, who worked in the forest sawmill with the machinery brought in sections from Turin.

Camisassa was trying to make clear to him that the brother (someone not a priest, that is to say) was every bit as true a missionary when working, if he did it in a spirit of faith. 'Do things as if you had Jesus beside you', he suggested. And he added, in connection with the Africans whom up till then he had never seen: 'They may look simple but they see everything, they observe everything, they do what you do. . . they study you from head to foot and they retain an impression that lasts for the rest of their lives.' Now the letter changes theme: 'I have sent you best quality mineral oil; it costs 4.50 lire a litre. There is also the Zimmermant type; it costs 5.50 lire a litre. Next, take care to position the morticer correctly; be careful to fasten the belts so that the spindle can never go into reverse; it is extremely dangerous. Then, tightly screw down the mortice iron, or else it will spin round and strike like a rifle bullet.' This was what the missionaries were told by the professor of Moral Theology and Canon Law, from the Consolata in Turin. Adding that: 'Reading your letter, the rector was very pleased indeed. . . The rector says as follows: Be an apostle by prayer and by example.' In the city caught up in the race to industrialization, the rector had good reason for keeping quiet as the bishops and cardinals filed past him in the Consolata during the centenary celebrations; he had had to put up with all sorts of things' being said about him, and now the temple was renovated. They would go on saying things about him, and he was now renovating people, from Turin to Africa, evangelizing with his little catechisms in Kikuyu and the morticer, with all those African eyes seeing all, observing everything.

The Venerable Joseph Cafasso

On 23 May 1906, Pope Pius X issued a decree ratifying the view of the Congregation of Rites (which in those days dealt with the causes of the saints), favouring the introduction of the apostolic process for the beatification of Fr Giuseppe Cafasso.

If we consider that Joseph Allamano was already active in this cause when Don Bosco was still alive (he died in 1888), a good many years have gone by. And more still will go by; for the beatification of the 'priest of the gallows' another twenty years are needed and two more popes, even though Pius X had expressed great satisfaction at seeing him on his way to the altars. The fact is that, for some saints, orders and religious congregations are at work or committees are set up, the help of bishops is invoked, the money is easier to find to defray the enormous work of documentation.

In Fr Cafasso's case there was none of this. Behind him, Fr Cafasso had only his nephew Joseph, his sister's son. And this nephew was supported only by Giacomo Camisassa. And this collateral story certainly deserves to be told: how the two of them succeeded in an undertaking that usually involves platoons of clergy and laity. The fact of the matter was that when the various enquiries were complete at diocesan level in Turin and all the documents had been laboriously copied out by hand and sent to Rome, this was only the beginning. In other words, the investigation had to begin all over again, but this time at the level of the universal Church. But there was nothing automatic about it. The mechanism could only be set in motion after the arrival of a sufficient number of written requests from members of Catholic reigning families, various authorities, cardinals, bishops; such was the message from Mgr Raffaele Virili, postulator of the cause, in Rome. Allamano and Camisassa then undertook this new chore too. 'With unconquered patience', one Catholic paper was to remark.

And the rector had to attend to all this in person, while guiding the missionaries in Africa, superintending the Pastoral Institute and finishing off the restoration work at the Consolata. For one moment he had dreamed that the introduction of the apostolic cause might have been announced in time for the centenary celebrations of 1904. Instead, he had to wait for two years. And then it was a matter of repeating, for the sake of the Vatican Congregation, the examination of many testimonies and acquiring more still; and more years would go by.

'The Church is immensely grateful to Canon Allamano, since to him and him alone the beatification of Fr Cafasso is due.' Such, when all was over, was the judgement of Cardinal Carlo Salotti, who had known all the ins and outs of the case. And Allamano, in the course of a spiritual talk to his own people one day, was to admit that on some evenings he was helpless with fatigue on leaving those Roman rooms.

Giuseppe Cafasso was his uncle, true; but the relationship in itself was not enough to account for thirty years of hard work and sacrifice for this beatification, which he was to see when virtually on the point of death. It was not a case of a kind of nepotism in reverse: we are faced with a precise plan which, Allamano considered, deserved all his efforts: to hold up to the entire Catholic clergy an up-to-date model of a priest, able once more to say persuasively to human beings that God loves them personally, and to encourage them with a vision of his mercy; a type of priest who does not run away from the hells of this earth but on the contrary frequents them to rescue the damned from them, by restoring hope, by despoiling even death of its terrifying connotations. 'If it had only been because Fr Cafasso was related to me, I would not have done all this,' he was to say one day. And again: 'Certainly I made all sorts of sacrifices! But I can honestly say I introduced this cause, not for reasons of affection or relationship, but for the good that can come from the exaltation of this holy priest.'

They were to find themselves face to face once more, Giuseppe Cafasso and Joseph Allamano, in May 1911. That is to say, at the end of that phase in the process which deals with the virtues and miracles of the 'Venerable'. At that point the procedure involves the examination of the tomb and the corpse. The event was recorded by G.B. Ressia, a student of the Pastoral Institute, as follows: 'At six o'clock in the evening, His Eminence the Cardinal Archbishop, Canon Allamano and all the members of the Commission, including the doctors of the process, entered the chapel of the Pastoral Institute. The *Veni Creator* was sung and the formula of the oath was read out. Then, as all the Pastoral Institute students observed, our rector's deep and holy joy could be seen, revealed in his face and in the movements of his body; and he had every reason! For this was the exaltation of someone who was at once his uncle and the Pastoral Institute's greatest glory!. . . The coffin containing the venerated corpse was carried on the Pastoral Institute students' shoulders. Among them, the rector had arranged, were all the ones from Castelnuovo. And it was placed in the hall where the bishops' conferences are held, and where it was opened the next morning.' More than half a century after death, the coffin was opened and the medical commission drew up its report on the condition of the body. The students of the Pastoral Institute and the Missionary Institute, and priests in great numbers, filed past the remains. As far as they were all concerned, Giuseppe Cafasso was already beatified and canonized.

Parish church of Sant'Andrea at Castelnuovo Don Bosco, Asti. (Photo: Fea)

View of Castelnuovo Don Bosco, birthplace of Joseph Allamano, St John Bosco, St Joseph Cafasso, Cardinal Giovanni Battista Cagliero, Giovanni Battista Bertagna, Auxiliary Bishop of Turin, and Matteo Filipello, Bishop of Ivrea. (Photo: Fea)

Pope John Paul II before the baptistry of the parish church at Castelnuovo (6 September 1988). Here were baptized Joseph Cafasso, 6 January 1811; John Bosco, 27 August 1815; and Joseph Allamano, 22 January 1851. (Photo: Felici)

Castelnuovo Don Bosco: Allamano family home and room where Blessed Joseph Allamano was born on 21 January 1851, the fourth of five sons. (Photo: Fea)

Marianna Cafasso (1813-1869), sister of St Joseph Cafasso, wife of Giovanni Allamano and mother of Blessed Joseph. He recalled how 'that holy woman my mother' 'had heavenly eyes'.

Kitchen of the Allamano house. Here the young Joseph met his uncle, the saint, for the only time in his life.

St Joseph Cafasso, in a painting by Enrico Reffo.

Above: *Family of the elder brother Giovanni Allamano (right) with his sons Pietro and Ottavio, daughter Paolina, wife Giuseppina Cafasso and elder daughter Benedetta.*
Below: *External view of the Major Seminary, Turin.*

Above: *Cloister of the Major Seminary, Turin.* Below: *Group photo from Joseph Allamano's years at the Seminary (about 1870). He is top row, second from right.*

Blessed Joseph Allamano in his early days as a priest.

Turin Cathedral with Guarini's cupola over the chapel of the Shroud. Joseph Allamano was ordained priest here on 20 September 1873 by Archbishop Lorenzo Gastaldi, and later became a canon. (Photo: Fea)

The venerable icon known as the Consolata.

The Shrine of the Consolata, of which Joseph Allamano was appointed rector in 1880. He stayed there for forty-six years until his death. (Photo: Fea)

Confessional box used by Blessed Joseph Allamano in the Shrine of the Consolata. (Photo: Rossi)

Canon Giacomo Camisassa (1854-1922), Joseph Allamano's first and loyal collaborator. Their priestly friendship was exemplary.

The Shrine of Sant'Ignazio near Lanzo, Turin; Joseph Allamano was rector of this and its attached retreat house.
(Photo: Baima)

Cardinal Agostino Richelmy (1850-1923), Archbishop of Turin, towards the end of his life. His friendship and support for Joseph Allamano were a decisive factor in the founding of the Missionary Institute.

The Pastoral Institute of the Consolata in Joseph Allamano's day. As rector, he re-opened it in 1882, meeting a need and righting what was a serious embarrassment for the diocese.

Above: *The Villa Allamano at Rivoli, a gift from Mgr Angelo Demichelis (1824-1898). From here, after his miraculous recovery in 1900, Joseph Allamano wrote for Cardinal Richelmy's permission to found the Institute. Below: Altar used by Joseph in the villa at Rivoli.* (Photo: Fea)

Joseph Allamano in his study in the villa at Rivoli.

Joseph Allamano surrounded by missionary students in the garden of the villa.

Above: *Original premises of the Consolata Missionary Institute, Turin, in the premises donated by Mgr Demichelis, 'La Consolatina'.* Below: *The present Mother House of the Consolata Missionaries.*

Above: *The first four Consolata missionaries to leave for Kenya: Tommaso Gays, Filippo Perlo, Luigi Falda and Celeste Lusso.* Below: *During their stay in Mombasa with the Vicar Apostolic, Emile Allgeyer.*

Above: *Group of Consolata Missionary Sisters in the early days of the Institute.* Below: *Arrival of the Consolata Missionary Sisters in Kenya, photographed with the Vincentian Sisters of the Cottolengo who had generously volunteered to serve with them.*

Filippo Perlo (1873-1948), the Institute's first Bishop, first Vicar Apostolic of Nyeri, succeeded Allamano as head of the Institute. He was the organizer of the Kenya mission.

A historic date in the progress of missionary activity in Kenya: the baptism of Chief Karuri (1916).

Blessed Joseph Allamano 'spoke to us and guided us with a perpetual smile on his face'.

Blessed Joseph Allamano photographed on the fiftieth anniversary of his ordination to the priesthood (1923).

Above: *The chest containing the mortal remains of Blessed Joseph Allamano.* (Photo: Rossi) Below: *Detail of the 'memorial room', in which some of his belongings are preserved. In the centre, the small picture of the Consolata, placed in his room during his serious illness of 1900. His cure, attributed to the Consolata's miraculous intervention, put an end to the delays over founding the Missionary Institute.*

Departure of the first four missionaries for Korea in 1987. The road opened by Joseph Allamano leads on.

The Church-Shrine of the Consolata, Nairobi, Kenya.

Consolata missionaries in Africa (above) and Latin America (below).

8

'We are independent'

On 12 September 1905, the Congregation of Propaganda Fide decreed the setting up of an 'independent mission' entrusted to the Consolata missionaries in the 'province of Kenya'; that is to say, in the Kikuyu territory where they were already working and which had thus been detached from Bishop Allgeyer's vicariate apostolic.

Fr Filippo Perlo was appointed superior, under the direct authority of the Holy See.

The decree put an end to the long and bitter controversy, which should never have broken out, between the evangelizers. We have already seen how the first Consolata missionaries, being as yet unable to install themselves among the Galla, had been accepted in the Vicariate as trainees, guests, collaborators of Bishop Allgeyer, all the while they were waiting to move into Galla territory. At a given moment, however, Allamano had made a different request. He put a proposal to the Vicariate and to the Congregation of the Holy Ghost that the Piedmontese missionaries' zone should be detached from the Vicariate, so as to start them on their way to a less provisional status. He hoped to make them into an independent Vicariate or at least a Prefecture Apostolic (in other words a territory already self-governing but still at an early stage of development, headed by a prefect without episcopal rank).

To the French missionaries all this seemed a violation of what had been agreed, a most disagreeable breach of faith. They very much appreciated the work of the Turin missionaries and were always happy to help them; but let there be no talk of ceding them that part of the Vicariate, or any other part for that matter. Indeed, in his boundless activities, Fr Filippo Perlo now and then was already venturing somewhat beyond his original field of work.

For Joseph Allamano, the request was justified on a variety of grounds based on one undeniable fact, also cordially praised by the French missionaries: the Consolata Institute was getting much better results than expected within its own zone. But this very success required unforeseen expenditure in sending out new missionaries to Africa as soon as possible and in adding to the equipment. This being the case, the Turinese Institute had to be able to rely on receiving its regular grants and contributions from its support organizations such as the Work for the Propagation of the Faith. But such organizations only gave regular subsidies to 'regular' missions, that is to say, those officially constituted, recognized, autonomous. . .

Since the mutual understanding suggested by Allamano could not be reached, recourse to Propaganda Fide was inevitable. And, in September 1905, the Congregation gave substantial satisfaction to the Consolata missionaries by making them independent, under the direct jurisdiction of the Holy See. It did not however concede the territory the rank of Vicariate or Prefecture Apostolic. An independent mission is something less. But at least the missionaries were now under their own roof.

The decree was published with the date of 14 September, the feast of the Exaltation of the Holy Cross, and a few days later Allamano informed the missionaries in Africa: 'With a heart filled with the liveliest joy, I send you the inspiring news that the Sacred Congregation *de Propaganda Fide* has erected the entire Province of Kenya into an Independent Mission entrusted to the Consolata missionaries. . . Few words, but they encompass a story of anxieties and lengthy negotiations, which have ended in a result exceeding my own expectations. Anxieties which have worried me for the last three years, for fear that the first field of your labours might be taken away from you, without my being able to foresee where the place destined by Providence to be the settled abode of my missionaries might be. . .'

The news made a strong impression in Turin too, where it then became clear to everybody that Cardinal Richelmy had been energetically supporting the missionaries' cause in Rome. Obviously, the Archbishop was not worried about losing diocesan priests. Many pessimists were now ready to change their tune: apparently the Consolata Mission in Africa was not going to be the 'flash in the pan' about which they had been grumbling. Perhaps — who could tell? — even Bishop Bertagna would have changed his mind, now that the Consolata missionaries had been taken up by the Vatican. But it did not happen in time for anyone to find out; he had died in February 1905. At his bedside had been Joseph Allamano, who happened not to see eye to eye with him but behaved with his invariable tact.

Bertagna his fellow-townsman, and Bishop Bertagna, one of the glories of Castelnuovo. . . One may well wonder what passed through Joseph Allamano's mind over this man's death and the settling of accounts that it implied. From boyhood days, he had seemed to live in the shadow of three glorious local figures: Fr Cafasso, Don Bosco and Bishop Bertagna. One wonders whether he realized that the children of Castelnuovo would in a sense be growing up in his own shadow now, with his former pupils spreading his reputation, with the newspapers writing about him, with the new missionary enterprise associated with his name. By this time, he too had reached the age of the glorious ones whom he used to admire as a child: fifty, fifty-five. He had already made history in the Turinese Church, he could slow down the rhythm, take things easier.

But fifty years earlier, the writer Goffredo Casalis had said that the country-folk of Castelnuovo, hospitable and cheerful, had little regard for their own health. Fr Cafasso used to say: 'We can do our resting in heaven', and he died at the age of forty-eight. Don Bosco: everybody had seen him dragging himself along on his swollen legs, to the discomfort of the doctors. ('But this man is dead already!' one of them exclaimed when visiting him.) And old Bertagna had insisted to go on teaching until he was at his last breath, and remain as rector of the seminaries, vicar general. . .

He would do the same. The independence of the mission was a satisfying goal. For other people, that is; for other types. No sooner had the commotion over his African enterprise begun to die down, than he behaved as though bent on re-activating it with a gust of novelty more foolhardy than the last.

This, in brief, was what he was preparing to do, after the 'declaration of independence'. First of all, to begin the transformation of the Institute into a proper religious congregation, with every member bound by vows instead of the oath required up to now. This involved another long Roman *iter*, with many visits and heavy correspondence, in order to pass through the successive stages to papal recognition. Meanwhile, he set aside the 'Piedmonticity' of the missionaries by opening the Institute to all. At the same time, he was to build new and impressive three-storey premises on a piece of land he had bought some time before in the meadows along Via di Circonvallazione, corresponding to present-day 44 Corso Ferrucci. With more space, it would be possible to have a junior seminary too, for little boys who aspired to become missionaries. Lastly, the biggest surprise of all: a female congregation. Allamano was going to have homemade missionary sisters as well.

He himself went on living at the Consolata, his command post: he would go down to the Pastoral Institute and find the future parish priests at work; he would go down to the Shrine where his people were waiting for him to hear their confessions. Others too would seek him out in the sacristy for advice, for help or to ask him to deal with some family problem. Or to give a votive picture for the Consolata. One of those little pictures (pencil and colour on paper) arrived from San Francisco in 1906: a Turinese woman escaped first from the terrible earthquake and then from the subsequent fire; and sent her thanks to the Consolata of Turin, signed 'Laura Fino' and the date of the catastrophe, '18 April 1906'.

So as to guide the Missionary Institute, he arranged his days like this: every Tuesday, Friday and Sunday, he goes there in person; on the other four days the prefect or other responsible people come and make their report to him. And of course, with Camisassa he is always to be found in the cathedral at the exact time the canons sing their Office. The engrained habit of rationing his time helps him never to arrive anywhere out of breath. He is always there with a minute to spare, with his usual 'gravity'. Who has ever seen him take the steps two at a time? And who would dare to do so under his mild and austere eye?

For urgent matters, he very soon had the telephone put in.

Of his three weekly visits to the Institute, the Sunday one was of special importance. There was the 'conference', a talk he used to give at the Institute on spiritual topics. One of the high moments in which he shaped new men: not merely those he had alive and attentive before him; not merely those. He was shaping those too whom he would never see, those yet to be born. He was also shaping some future martyr whose name he did not know. Joseph Allamano did not leave any ascetical writings, treatises, tomes for the future instruction of his children. He left them himself, poured into these 'talks' in a very simple, homely Italian, with his soft voice never rising in tone.

For, while he spoke, his words were accurately taken down, Sunday by Sunday. A little group of seven priests was formed for the purpose. Rather like what used to happen at Valdocco with the 'secret commission', little by little recording the sayings of Don Bosco. Only here there was nothing secret. And every now and then, the rector would collate the text taken down by the copyists with his own notes. For these talks too were rigorously prepared, in spite of often seeming informal improvizations on events or old memories, or commemorations of individuals, reflections on religious feasts. All these various literary genres were in fact his vehicles for lessons in theology, morality, asceticism, the voice of the prophets and evangelists, missionary problems. The *summa* of his teaching is contained entirely in these recorded talks: more than seven hundred, not counting a few dozen others addressed to the young aspirants for the missions. On these pages, other evangelizers too were to shape themselves after he was dead.

New house, big house

On the land bought in what is now Corso Ferrucci (the vendors were the Jewish family of Sacerdote), building began in 1906 or 1907; there is some discrepancy over the date. On an area of twelve thousand square metres was to rise a large, three-storey structure, suited to the new requirements. It had to accommodate the seminary for the missions, the novitiate, the boarding school for the young candidates, and of course the church and complementary premises. G. Mina and L. Zamuner write soberly: 'Raising the money is not proving easy for Allamano at a time when the missions have absorbed almost everything he has. Meanwhile, he decides to sell some valuables received as a gift from a benefactress; Providence will do the rest.' The financial situation got more critical as the work proceeded, obliging him and Giacomo Camisassa to strip themselves virtually of all they had and to impose economies 'on the very customary things of life', as Fr Sales observes. In particular, the rector was even to sell his little house, 'La Morra', between Castelnuovo and Moncucco, purchased towards the end of the century for 60,000 lire and sold on to two nephews for 42,500.

Canon Camisassa re-lived field days of old, being able to get back on to a building site, climbing up the scaffolding, finding fault with the materials: 'Not Dora sand! I want Stura sand in the plaster. Stura, do you hear! Dora sand makes nasty spots appear, once you begin distempering. . .' The sight of that cassock arriving at the works spread no joy among the bricklayers, master-builders, artisans, architects. At times, the harshness of the disagreements required Allamano to intervene with all his abilities as a mediator. It even reached a stage of written polemic, like the one with the master-carpenter Giovanni Caneparo. Let us allow him to speak for a moment, since he is very representative of a hard-working world revolving round the Consolata in a Turin which at that very moment was seeing firms like Lancia come into being, and the future Officine Moncenisio, and the future Riv, while an Itala car of Turinese manufacture astonished the world in the Peking-Paris Expedition.

This then is how that Turin would express itself, in a letter from Caneparo to Camisassa, before the work started: 'At the Institute for the Missions I intend to do the job as though the house were my own, and I want people to say a hundred years from now that the carpenter who made those windows really knew what he was doing.' And he adds with quiet pride: if to save money the work were to be entrusted to other people, 'I shall not be offended and I shall always be Caneparo of the Consolata. I am not short of work. . .'

When then, once the work was in progress, Camisassa was to find fault with him (wrongly, it would seem) over the measurements of some doors, this was his reply: he had cut the doors in a certain way 'with forty years' experience in the trade and thirty-one as owner of the workshop', being used to working 'according to the building customs of Turin, where we live, and not in some ideal world. . . No architect, no master-builder, no proprietor has ever made the *strange* observations to me that you have. . . Do you understand? Prove me wrong if you can.'

This more than frank exchange between authoritative theologian and respected carpenter is a telling sign of the intermingling of clerical and popular components in the Consolata world (Shrine and Institute) in Allamano's day. That such a rapport was reached was largely due to him, who knew better than others how to tap the vitality of the populace. In the Shrine, there was a traditional link with the aristocracy, with the royal family, and this he respected and preserved, but without making it exclusive either. With him, the Turin of the trades and the work-shops, now facing an industrial future, had learnt (or re-learnt) the feeling of being at home under those sacred vaults. The Company of the Consolata, for centuries reserved for patricians, was opened, thanks to him, to people of every social class.

Still in this spiritual field: certain 'pious unions' dedicated to the Consolata came into existence: expressions of the world of labour; their members were drawn for instance from the work-force of the tobacco manufactures of the Royal Park, and those of textile companies such as Bass & Abrate and the Poma cotton mill. Again, the Franchetti sisters created the Consolata Workshop — making women's clothing — with this aim: 'To give a Christian training to dressmakers, who then in their turn, having themselves become employers of dressmakers, may observe the day of rest and thus remove, or at least somewhat diminish, the scourge so deeply rooted especially in the dressmaking class: the profanation of holy days.' Day of rest, less oppressive working hours, holidays in the mountains for sickness, a sort of pension: such were the new features of this workshop,

111

of which the women-initiators were to say after more than thirty years' activity: 'Without Canon Allamano, the workshop would never have been founded. . . And not a few of the clergy, many of them very devout ones too, were opposed to it. . .'

And this is the world to which the expert and frank carpenter Caneparo also belongs; and this is why he can talk in this way to the vice rector of 'his' Consolata! Furthermore he has a son, Aquilino, in Canon Allamano's African Missions. Some years later, he himself, a widower, was to become a religious at Moncalieri in the Congregation of the Blessed Sacrament, taking the name Bro. Giuseppe.

The new house was needed, and urgently too, because Canon Allamano in 1907 had announced something new: the Consolata Missionary College for Boys (later known as St Paul's Junior Seminary). The first little group of six was to arrive in November the following year and still be housed in the building in Corso Duca di Genova, the 'Consolatina'. As time passed, many more were to come, more than foreseen; and not all cut out for the missionary life, as will be seen. Accompanying them to see him, parents and parish priests must have been rather taken aback at his methods: he examined and questioned the candidates with almost mistrustful care. He disillusioned some of them. He briskly disappointed those who showed any sign of thinking missionary life was a springboard to adventure. (Adventure was in fashion in Turin, those years: they had seen Leon Delagrange flying, who was very short; Colonel Cody, alias Buffalo Bill, who was very old and had come from New York with Red Indians and horses. . .) No go. Religious ardour and a yearning for faraway lands did not constitute 'a clear sign of vocation to the missions', so it was better to forget it. Even those who got accepted were laid under a definite obligation to speak up quickly and clearly, should they later perhaps feel less keen on the idea: 'The College. . . has one sole aim: the training of suitable lads to be priests and brothers, holy missionaries. Any other aim would be against truth and justice, and they would be falling short in those if, on becoming aware of not being called to our missions, they did not raise the matter with the superiors immediately.'

He wanted quality, not numbers, just as Camisassa wanted Stura sand, not Dora. In both cases, if immediate care was not taken, nasty spots would come out later. The wicket was open to anyone wanting to come in; the main gates were thrown wide for anyone wanting to depart; this was his philosophy as regards candidates for missionary work. Having only a few people did not worry him; what alarmed him was the idea of a hodgepodge, in other words light-heartedly accepting people to raise the numbers and hoping for the best. One day, after the founding of the Sisters, Cardinal Cagliero, a fellow-countryman and friend of the Canon's, came to pay them a visit. This was what one sister recalled: 'The Cardinal was surprised at seeing there were so few of us and, walking among us, said: "There are too few of you; you must attract others; do some advertising." Behind him came Allamano who looked at us and signalled No, with his raised finger.'

What was wanted was not advertising but lucidity. Everyone had to know one could not become a good missionary without first sanctifying oneself; this was the order of priorities. You were not a missionary merely because you wanted to, because you knew or thought you knew the techniques of persuasion; in other words, you considered yourself a missionary-born by virtue solely of being white and stepped in white culture. Here too Canon Allamano raised his finger, signalling No. First, personal sanctification: or, in other words, acceptance in full of kinship in God with the African, in the style of Paul the Apostle, for whom 'there cannot be Greek and Jew, circumcised and uncircumcised, barbarian, Scythian, slave, free man, but Christ is all, and in all' (Col 3:11). This then meant studying, knowing and respecting the native culture of the African as being suitable, like any other, to accept the Christian offer and develop within it in accordance with African intelligence and creativity.

The message persuades then, if accompanied by a sincere and faithful effort to promote human values by means of work. Work is not preaching; work teaches materially by showing how things are done. Even the sawmill in the Kenyan forest evangelizes in its own way. Therefore let the future missionaries understand that their training in Turin will have to entail activities that include manual and technical work. 'Yours is not a life of ecstacy, it is a life of work. Working as St Paul worked, to earn his own keep and to do good to others, while devoting himself to their salvation. You must work as willingly out of doors as indoors; in the appointed time, let each qualify in a trade.' Cardinal Massaia was both tailor and cobbler to his Ethiopians; and Don Bosco was as much for the first Valdocco boys.

Victory in Rome and in Africa

In 1907 after two years of 'independent mission', Joseph Allamano furnished Propaganda Fide with documents on the development of the work in Kenya. And he asked that on the ecclesiastical level the territory might be promoted to the rank of Vicariate Apostolic (skipping the intermediate phase of being a Prefecture). But Rome, which on other occasions had been so speedy, this time gave no response, let months and then a year go by and still said nothing. In Turin they were worried, and in Africa too. Allamano got his Roman friends to work and the reason for the silence then came to light: they had lost the file. It was probably under a pile of papers in the office of Cardinal Gotti, the learned and extremely courteous Prefect of Propaganda Fide. A duplicate was sent from Turin, and everything speeded up. After the Congregation's vote in favour, dated 28 June 1909, Pius X gave his ratification on the following 6 July: the 'independent mission' became the Vicariate Apostolic of Kenya, and there now had to be a Bishop to rule it. He was to be Fr Filippo Perlo, the present superior.

The new bishop left Africa, arriving in Turin towards the end of August, and on 9 September was received in audience with Canon Allamano by Pius X, later giving an account of this in *La Consolata* bulletin: 'When we had explained that our apostolate did not consist exclusively in catechizing but that, as an introduction to and in parallel with this, we concerned ourselves with the health and material of the poor blacks, whether by looking after the sick and importing new kinds of foodstuffs, or by getting them used to working and wearing clothes, His Holiness gave as it were a sigh of satisfaction: "Make them into men, make them hardworking and then you will have good Christians too." '

On Saturday 23 October 1909, in the Shrine of the Consolata, Cardinal Richelmy, Valfré di Bonzo, Archbishop of Vercelli, and Giovanni Tasso, Bishop of Aosta, consecrated Filippo Perlo who was then thirty-six, in the presence of his two missionary brothers, Gabriele and Luigi. The first people he saw kneeling before him for his blessing were Joseph Allamano and Giacomo Camisassa, who was the new bishop's uncle on his mother's side.

This was also the date on which the large new house was inaugurated in Corso Ferrucci, and the chronicles of the Consolata speak (perhaps for the only time in Joseph Allamano's lifetime) of a 'solemn lunch'. This was both to fete the new Bishop and to marvel over the hugeness of the new building in comparison with the 'Consolatina' ('where we kept bumping into one another', as the rector once remarked). Here there was enough room for the hundred pupils of the junior seminary, the twenty students of the novitiate and some fifty students of the major seminary. From the time when already-ordained priests flocked into the premises in Corso Duca di Genova, we have now reached the times when the Consolata makes missionaries on its own premises.

At the end of the same year 1909 there was another victory bulletin. The Consolata Missionary Institute, now structured as a religious congregation, had received the *Decretum laudis* from Rome. And this was the first of a series of approvals spaced out in time, until the final one. Its importance lay in the fact that it promoted the institution, transferring it from diocesan to pontifical jurisdiction and conferring on it citizenship of the entire, universal Church, owing obedience to the Holy See and no longer to an individual bishop. The decree furthermore confirmed the appointment of Joseph Allamano as Superior General for six years, with Camisassa as his Vicar General. They were now under the jurisdiction of the Congregation for Religious, a situation not without its drawbacks for a missionary association. Allamano was now to take the necessary steps to return to being under the more logical jurisdiction of Propaganda Fide.

To make victory complete, all that could have been wished for would have been the approval of the Institute's new Constitutions. That however would still be a matter of time, correspondence, meetings. But for the time being, there was something else of enormous importance. Pope Pius X had of his own authority approved and praised the Institute's *missionary method*. On 10 October, Joseph Allamano was able to send a copy of the Pope's words to all the missionaries in Africa: 'The need is to make hardworking people of the natives, so as to be able to make them Christians: to show them the benefits of civilization so as to draw them to love the faith; they will love a religion which, as well as promising them a future life, also makes them happier on earth.'

Allamano had his reasons for divulging the Pope's good opinion, for the 'Consolata method' had aroused disapproval among many of the clergy. He spoke of this himself to his people in Africa: 'In the past, people took it upon themselves to criticize our evangelizing method, as though we were too concerned with material at the expense of spiritual welfare; it was said that what was needed was to preach and baptize and not bother about anything else.' Many people however have changed their opinion; for himself, he enthusiastically returns to his first model, Matteo Ricci, 'who, to enter China and win respect for himself and his missionaries and so open the way to converting those people, began by teaching mathematics, by constructing terrestrial globes and sundials: things that made him esteemed and well-deserving, and then believed as regards what he taught about the Christian faith. To those in Europe who criticized him for wasting time by spending it in the secular sciences, he replied: "I for myself set more store by this than having made ten thousand Christians." And in fact, even though during his own lifetime only two thousand Christians were baptized, God's word reached many millions of pagans, and only a few years after his death Christians already numbered forty thousand.'

Matteo Ricci, China, missionary method. . . It also must be said that in the year 1910 the top ranks of the Church were by no means yet in accord over praising that Jesuit and the way he evangelized the Chinese. There were still

116

another thirty years to go before Pius XII put a stop to the protracted diatribe, and further years before the Fathers of the Second Vatican Council would encourage — shall we say in the Allamano style? — 'the wasting of time on secular sciences' by recommending to the faithful at large: 'Let them blend modern science and its theories and the understanding of the most recent discoveries with Christian morality and doctrine. Thus their religious practice and morality can keep pace with their scientific knowledge and with an ever-advancing technology. . . Through a sharing of resources and points of view, let those who teach in seminaries, colleges and universities try to collaborate with men well versed in other sciences' (*Gaudium et Spes* 62).

The people Allamano was writing to in Africa already knew his views, since in the 'conferences' he constantly returned to the topic with quotations and similes: 'St Francis de Sales used to say that knowledge is the eighth sacrament'; 'an ignorant priest is an image of sadness and disappointment, for the anger of God and the desolation of the people. For he has a mouth for proclaiming God's word, but because of his ignorance he keeps it shut, and this is the lesser of two evils, for if he spoke, he would give voice to error. . . Similarly, an ignorant missionary is an image of sadness and disappointment for the Institute.'

In the letter to the missionaries, exhortation has become affectionate statement of fact; 'But why do I say these things to you when you willingly spend months and years in a sawmill or a factory, never growing tired, always being content and sure of thus best doing your apostolate? You understand perfectly well that, for the time being, real preaching would be useless, that God's word must be sown in a more gentle, almost casual way during work, and with frequent stints of catechesis. . .'

Giacomo Camisassa often had the job of expanding into elegant form and writing the exhortations springing forth from daily conversations with the rector. If this was how things were even then, as regards the message to the people in Africa, he may have wondered: is the rector only speaking of Matteo Ricci, or also of me?

The rector had in fact had some bad moments at the end of 1909 and beginning of 1910, when it became known that

Rome wanted to send Camisassa to a Piedmontese diocese as bishop. In the Vatican everyone had come to know him, from Pius X downwards, and someone had thought of him as bishop, asking the sub-Alpine episcopate for the usual information. We do not know what the two of them said to each other on the subject in the course of their daily conversations, but they found themselves in agreement on a resolute refusal; Allamano appealed to old Roman friends, and in some degree the Archbishop of Turin also lent a hand by describing Camisassa to Rome as one endowed with all the gifts of a good bishop, save one: a sense of fatherhood. So no episcopate and no separation: business as before. Joseph Allamano had three more years of him, and had always thought of him as his natural successor at the head of the Missionary Institute. He even made an unusual request to the Congregation for Religious: to put the Institute under the leadership not of one but of two Superiors General, Allamano-Camisassa — a kind of consulate as in ancient Rome. It was one way of fixing the succession in advance, there and then. The Holy See did not agree and Camisassa remained 'Vice'; everyone knew however about the absolute trust existing between the two men, so that the succession, rather than in Vatican decrees, seemed already written in the facts. No one knew at that point that of the two, the younger would be the one to die first.

9

An appeal to the Pope

'I was struck by his very dignified restraint, by his expression which was much out of the ordinary. . . I realized this was the priest about whom my own parish priest had spoken to me and I was convinced the opinion expressed by my parish priest with regard to him was fully in accordance with the truth: that he was indeed a holy priest.'

These are the words of Maria Demaria of Dronero, who in October 1910 became one of the earliest Consolata Missionary Sisters and who, known in religion as Sr Margherita, was destined to become their Superior General. In this reminiscence, we find confirmation of the impression that the person of Joseph Allamano was already making on people at a first meeting. Furthermore, the reference to the parish priest of Dronero is significant, indicating as it does the respect in which the rector was held even outside the diocese, his reputation for sanctity having been spread by the parochial tom-tom: people who met him at the Pastoral Institute, or at the Consolata, or at retreats. And this 'very dignified' appearance which struck young Maria Demaria, his way of speaking, his amiable brotherly gestures, all combined to produce that conclusive judgement, ever more widely diffused: he was a holy priest.

The attraction exerted by Joseph Allamano's person also helps to explain the success of the new undertakings he threw himself into, now that he was sixty: the creation, no less, of a missionary congregation for women.

The time was not to prove favourable, since there were complaints already in the Church over the excessive numbers of sisters, and the Holy See had set its face — first with Leo XIII, now with Pius X — to discourage new foundations. But for the Consolata Institute the need was getting serious and urgent. With the expansion of evangelization in Africa, requests for female personnel were increasing, and the Cottolengo was certainly in no position to send any more religious. And furthermore there were tricky and even unpleasant problems.

We have already seen the Vincentian Sisters from the Cottolengo going from village to village, tending the sick, stooping over the most revolting sores, struggling with the scourge of jiggers burrowing underneath their toenails. They were wonderful and by now, as well as the missionaries, thousands and thousands of Africans were grateful to them for looking after them and curing them. But this was it: Bishop Perlo said they were marvellous 'make-shift doctors' but not trained for other mission tasks, such as for instance catechizing in the local language. Which was of course true: they had joined the Cottolengo for a different vocation, in which they had then been trained and which they then performed. Going to Africa had been a surprise to which they had willingly adjusted with all the required dedication. However, this did not seem to tally with the plans of the Vicar Apostolic, Filippo Perlo, whose strategy offered the sisters ample scope, provided they put themselves under his jurisdiction. The hyperactive bishop needed obedient subordinates.

Now this obviously could not be reconciled with the Vincentian Sisters' very strong and logical attachment to their own particular inspiration, to the Cottolengo charism and to the autonomy of one religious family hurrying to the aid of another but certainly not to be subjugated and absorbed.

The Cottolengo could not therefore send any more sisters. Also, after all those years of very valuable activity, the ones in Africa were to be recalled. Joseph Allamano looked about him at orders and congregations of ancient and modern date. But he could not find one able to furnish female religious specifically trained for missionary work, particularly missionary work in Africa. He realized there was only one right solution: to train them at home himself. Also because it had already happened that some girls had tried to get admitted to the Consolata Institute, off their own bat, not knowing that the Institute was exclusively for men. For instance, a girl called Gabriella Bertino turned up from Ceva with an introduction from the rector of the local orphanage, Fr

Giovanni Torelli, another priest whom Joseph Allamano's reputation for holiness had reached.

In a word, the only thing left was to sound out Rome, present the case, test the pulse of Propaganda Fide. And this was what the rector and Filippo Perlo did in September 1909 on their journey to Rome after the erection of the Vicariate Apostolic. They spoke to Cardinal Gotti about it, who naturally knew all about the coldness prevailing over new sisters. But it was also true that in this case it was a matter of specialists, of missionaries, who certainly were not thick on the ground. They also spoke about it at the audience granted to Allamano and the new Bishop by Pius X. And the upshot of the matter was that the two returned from Rome, encouraged to go ahead.

So, on 29 January 1910, the Institute of Consolata Missionary Sisters came into being, housed in Corso Duca di Genova at the still unoccupied 'Consolatina'. Or to be more accurate, the Institute came into being in a manner of speaking, since at that date there were only Sr Celestina Bianco and Sr Dorotea Marchisio of the Congregation of the Sisters of St Joseph, called in to get the work started. These two, and that was all. You could even say that this institute of sisters came into existence without any sisters.

But then they started arriving: there were seven of them by mid-May, fifteen within the year, more than thirty in 1911. There could have been more but Allamano did not abate his rigour in selecting them. Indeed, if anything he increased it, well knowing what awaited these women in Africa. And the results were not long to seek: either in the number of those who were to go all the way, or in the quality; for, of the 'first entrants', two were to become Superiors General: Sr Margherita Demaria of Dronero and Sr Maria degli Angeli Vassallo of Turin. The training was rigorous too, to which the rector devoted himself in person with his regular presence and the famous and very effective 'talks': of which three hundred and thirty-seven were to be transcribed and preserved.

The Institute of Consolata Missionary Sisters was developing in another very active period for Turin. 1911 marked the fiftieth anniversary of the Kingdom of Italy and this was celebrated in the former capital in a manner never seen before, that is to say, with a Universal Exhibition destined to go down in the history of Turin and Italy as a unique event. Never had there been, and never in the twentieth century would there be, an exhibition in Italy on such a scale. And never did such an exhibition close down in credit, having paid off every penny borrowed and even with a small 'dividend' into the bargain. Unfortunately however 1911 also saw the start of the Libyan War, which broke out on 29 September 1911 and came to an end with the Treaty of Ouchy on 18 October 1912. (Various *ex-votos* from soldiers in Libya reached the Consolata during this period; and below the vaulting of the Shrine, one by one, may be read the names of the places and the battles: Derna, Zanzur, Azizia, Gargaresh.)

In the peaceful month of October, the sisters moved from the 'Consolatina' to the big building in Corso Ferrucci, which from then on was to be called the Mother House for everyone. In the new headquarters, they also replaced the Sisters of San Gaetano in doing the housework. They now also had their own habit (the first clothing occurred in October 1910), thought up by Allamano, Camisassa and a well-known dressmaker in Turin, Signora Giovanna Maria Rosanno, who had previously undertaken other jobs for the Consolata and the Pastoral Institute. Allamano did not want the usual black clothes, so they went for grey ('since in Africa too it will not show the dirt').

Then, in 1913, three events occurred which brought the new Institute into the forefront of evangelizing. At the beginning of April, the first eleven sisters made their religious profession. On 11 May, Sr Celestina Bianco of the Josephite Sisters gave up her job as initiator and the Consolata Sisters had their own, first, superior; she was Sr Margherita Demaria, appointed by the rector; to her, in order to overcome his own anxieties, he provisionally gave the title of Vice Superior. He himself was the superior, with all the responsibilities. And at last, on 3 November 1913, the first group set out: fifteen sisters with three missionaries left Turin for Africa. At Porta Nuova Station, the rector blessed them and handed them a letter which was, as it were, the final chapter in his work of training them. It contained a statement of the goal they had to reach ('To make yourselves holy and with yourselves to save many souls') and the means for arriving at it, which are the religious and apostolic virtues, and particularly 'the spirit of faith, of obedience, of charity and of mortification.' His Monferrato realism then helped him in pointing out the means for extracting themselves from the crises that each of them would inevitably have to face: 'Just as I do not think you are perfect yet with that perfection you will only acquire in heaven, so I heartily exhort you not to be discouraged by your, even repeated, faults; examine them and humble yourselves, if they are public ones, before the superior and the sisters every evening; and if it is a case of lack of charity towards the sisters, then do so the moment you have fallen.'

'If only the Pope would take action. . .'

These departures for Africa, as Joseph Allamano saw them, were not a fine and moving act on the part of the Institute, not of the Institute alone. He always saw them as acts of the Turinese Church as such — he himself was a diocesan priest and would never wish to be anything else — in its natural missionary dimension. Hence the gatherings of the faithful at the Consolata, with the Archbishop; hence the solemnity of the services and the choral leave-taking of those departing for Africa: from his point of view, at these moments the Church of Turin was entirely true to herself. He also had the good fortune, in Cardinal Richelmy, to find a natural sensitivity to the problem. But lucky coincidences were not enough for him and nor was the horizon of Turin.

The man who was able to devote time and energy to the problems of the individual boy in the college, of the individual sister, thought of missionary work on the scale of the universal Church. He was scandalized by what might be called communities' and their pastors' amnesia as regards the duty of 360° evangelization, far beyond the limits of parish and diocese. 'The entire Church is a mission and the work of evangelization is God's people's basic duty.' A Council fifty years later was to remind God's people about this, but he for his part had always thought so and would never stop thinking so. 'All Bishops, being members of the episcopal body that succeeded the apostolic college, have been consecrated not merely for the diocese, but for the salvation of the whole world': this, as well, fifty years later! And he not only thought it but sensed that something out of the ordinary was needed, to replant the idea in everyone's head.

All very fine, right, effective to go the rounds giving missionary talks with slides sent home by Bishop Perlo. This was being done all over the place by various orders, congregations, institutes, with slides from every continent. But something quite different was needed, Joseph Allamano would say to himself and to Canon Camisassa. What was absolutely necessary was a general shake-up, a really dramatic one, for the whole Catholic Church. And naturally the Pope was the one to give it, vested in all his authority as head of the apostolic college at present in office on earth. He alone could put an end to the scandal of Bishops who, in practice, sabotaged missionary initiatives merely because they were afraid of losing a junior curate or a seminarian or two; and the other scandal of an entire teaching Church's taking care not to teach anything about the missions and those who work in them, as though afraid that people should know too much about them.

Right then, the Pope must be brought into it. And so, on 29 August 1912, the rector wrote to five superiors of Italian missionary institutes: Bishop Conforti of Parma, Fr Vianello of Verona, Fr Viganò of Milan, Fr Traverso of Genoa and Fr Callerio of Rome. It did not take him many words to describe a situation with which they were familiar: in Italy there was massive ignorance about missions, general apathy among clergy and faithful, a scarcity of specialized vocations, partly because these were openly discouraged by the bishops. And so, he suggested, we must get the Pope to take action: 'One way. . . would be an official act of the Supreme Pontiff in which he placed the Work of the Apostolate among the heathen in its true light, exhorted all the faithful and especially the clergy to support it and, above all, exhorted the Bishops not only to refrain from obstructing but actually to support vocations to the apostolate among their clergy and their flock.' And he urged: we could take advantage of a forthcoming occasion, the sixteenth centenary of Constantine's edict granting freedom to the Church, which was to be celebrated in 1913.

By doing this, Joseph Allamano, he of the charming manners and soft voice, steps boldly forward to indict the whole Italian Church in its Bishops, with the clarity of a prophet, neither sweetening nor toning down his message. Yes, with the courage to summon the Pope himself to action; to tell him too, in substance, that the Italian Church is in a state of non-performance, unfaithful to her mandate.

The five recipients of the letter vigorously supported his suggestion. A document was consequently drawn up, addressed to Pius X, in the form of a petition, repeating — in highly respectful language, it must be confessed — all the accusations in the letter to the five and then formulating a request: that the Supreme Pontiff, by his own authority, would institute a Mission Sunday to be held annually 'with the obligation of a sermon on the duty and methods of propagating the faith throughout the world'; and then these dioceses, these parishes, will have to pull themselves together!

But the document met with various accidents on its course. First, the Congregation of Propaganda Fide refused to give it official support with the Pope. Then the signatories made a further mistake when, instead of presenting the petition themselves 'in person' to Pius X, they had it delivered by Fr Callerio on his own, since he resided in Rome. And he for his part did his duty but was unable to see the Pope, who was tied up with the Christmas ceremonies; so he delivered the document to his secretary, Fr Bressan.

The Pope's physical strength was declining and his mind besides was full of anxiety over the danger to peace. In February 1912, two years of strife had begun in the Balkans; the arsenals of Europe were stocked full. He himself, when the Brazilian ambassador took leave of him before going home in the early days of 1913, had said to him: 'You are lucky you will not be involved in the war.' That is to say, the general European conflict; the 'great war' as he sometimes called it.

This was the state of mind the Pope was in when he read the denunciation and Joseph Allamano's proposal in the petition. And he hastened to respond to it, on 31 January

1913, not with a document addressed to the Church, nor to the Bishops but with a reply only to the six of them, agreeing about the great duty of missionary work and praising them 'for the care you take in training teams of evangelizers'. But he did not say a word about the responsibility of the Bishops (nor perhaps could he say anything on that score in a letter addressed to third parties). And similarly, he said nothing about the suggestion of instituting a Mission Sunday. (The Vatican bureaucracy compounded all this with a contribution of its own, by even messing up the promoter's name and address, which appears on the envelope as 'Canon *Alemanno*, Superior of the *Immacolata* Missionaries'.)

Discouraging but nothing to lose heart over. In spite of the little said, in his letter Pius X did talk about the missions; so, instead of cherishing disappointment and resentment, he concentrated on disseminating and commenting on the document, thus making use of it to the maximum in the work of arousing enthusiasm for the missions. When faced with resistance on the verge of sabotage, it was important to be able to flourish this sheet of paper with Pius X's signature on it.

What Joseph Allamano was now so quick to understand and proclaim, with the risks that foresight incurs, others were to understand later. The shake-ups for the Church would come later: first with the Apostolic Brief *Maximum Illud* of Benedict XV in 1919, and then with the Encyclical *Rerum Ecclesiae* of Pius XI in 1926. And the said Pius XI was to have the first World Mission Sunday observed in 1927.

Meanwhile not one word, not one sigh, of disappointment over Pius X was to escape him. Above all because he knew how much he owed to him in the field of missionary activity itself. And then because he was not, and never would be, a man to shift the blame on to someone else. Humble and hidden in ordinary moments and festivities as he might be, he yielded place to no one when it came to shouldering responsibilities: then he calmly says 'I', describes himself as 'founder' without pleasure and without fear, loading his own shoulders with all possible and most disagreeable pieces of luggage, while preserving not only his faith but his style as well. In the end, many people spoke of him as being

126

a man of absolute faith. Not a passive faith however, not merely waiting. Faith that was bound up with a quiet conscience: I have done everything I can, I have not wasted a moment nor dogged an effort, now it is up to Someone Else to act.

At the same time he was accumulating an exceptionally rich experience of human nature, which helped him to see clearly in situations from which there sometimes seemed to be no way out, and to make rational forecasts which some people regarded as virtually prophetic. Fr James Alberione, the founder of the Society of St Paul and the Daughters of St Paul, for the apostolate through the media of social communication, went more than once to ask his advice and left this account of him: 'His intuition and soundness of judgement were admirable; when I went to him, he would not need to let me finish speaking, a word or two were enough for him and he answered with such simplicity, brevity and conviction as inspired one with courage to take action, and peace of mind. I always had the feeling there was something more than the light of nature within him; all the more so since, when put into effect, I always found his advice to have been good. . . I heard him give advice on the vocation of two young seminarians: he had only had the briefest moment to hear what they had to say; he grasped the situation immediately and gave his opinion. It was not followed, since other people had judged differently. In the special circumstances, the serenity with which he then adapted himself was admirable, so that the contrary opinion should be followed, given by someone inexpert, young and self-opinionated. But his own advice turned out to have been absolutely right: things fell out to the letter as he said they would. . . Later and after moral damage had been done, the way had to be taken as Canon Allamano had pointed out. . . I still wonder whether he had not then had some special intuition.'

Intuition, or perhaps inspiration. This is certainly not a subject within the chroniclers' realm, all the more so since He who inspires usually proceeds by unforeseen and curious ways. There is however one thing certain: Giuseppe Allamano's readiness for what today we call total absorption as regards individuals, or problems, or situations.

Whereas he had to recognize the damage caused by Italian listlessness where missionary work was concerned, he instantly grasped the importance of the blacks in Africa not only as receivers but as spreaders of the faith. After decades of living among only Piedmontese priests, Piedmontese seminarians, the Piedmontese faithful, Piedmontese sins and omissions, Joseph Allamano arrived at an understanding of African missionary problems with the sureness of someone who had prepared himself by years of specialized research. Because he had indeed determined to immerse himself in the subject and make it his. Thus he quickly learned what the Western colonists still did not know or did not want to know; he learned that the future of the mission to the blacks lay with the blacks themselves. And he instantly assigned this rich priority to the Consolata missionaries: training black catechists as quickly as possible.

'It should be everyone's business to cooperate in training them, preparing them with care and special study at the mission station before sending them to the college (the central school for catechists). And, when they come back, loving them and making them part, as it were, of the family circle; instructing them with a short talk every day; making them enthusiastic about their work; getting them into the habit, by reporting every evening, of keeping themselves informed about what is happening in the country, about the sick, about foundlings; making use of them, not overlooking them and not wasting their time with other jobs. In a word, concentrating as much care on them as you can, so that they will live sober, devout lives, absorbed in their work. It is a fact. . . that missions are happy and productive where the catechists are happy and hardworking.'

Kenya: the Vice Rector's visit

Allamano wrote and spoke as though he had been in Africa to see, yet he was never to go there; he was father of missionaries, never having seen a single mission: spiritual father to countless new African Christians but at long range, from Turin. For him to go travelling in such places was very unadvisable, now that he was over sixty, in his state of health. From Kenya, Bishop Perlo advised strongly against such an adventure.

So the African visit was performed by Giacomo Camisassa in his full capacity as vice rector and Allamano's personal representative, with the approval of the Congregation of Propaganda Fide, and with his own passion for seeing people and things from close quarters: the Vicar Apostolic who was also his nephew, the ordained and lay missionaries, the Vincentian Sisters and then the workshops, the machinery in the forest, the Pelton turbine in action. . .

He left on 8 February 1911, after making his will (Allamano being the sole beneficiary), with another of his nephews, Fr Gabriele Perlo, and with Aquilino, son of Caneparo the carpenter. The rector bade them farewell at Porta Nuova Station and for Camisassa that leave-taking was 'a wrench': so long a separation after such close daily contact for thirty-one years, since the day in fact when the twenty-six-year-old priest from Caramagna was supposedly on his way to be junior curate at Pecetto.

For a long while now, letters would take the place of conversation, with exchanges of news and comparison of views, just as when they used to talk each day, and with anxious moments as after the news of Allamano's fevers during a visit to Rome at the end of 1911, provoking this response from Camisassa: 'For heaven's sake look after yourself properly, especially during the winter months, which are always bad for you, coming and going to the cathedral and your duties there with all those draughts outside and in choir. . .'

The journey was supposed to last until November 1911 but was in fact extended until April 1912 on account of all the things to be seen and examined and on account of some new things in addition. Moving from one missionary settlement to another with Bishop Perlo, he saw the signs of his energetic hand and of his enterprising skill in bringing things to fruition, and in the welcome they received from place to place from the blacks. And he filled his notebooks with technical observations to be sent as fast as possible to Turin: to train some furnace-men and stone masons; have samples of Kenyan earth analyzed for eventual use in building. . . .

Now at last before his eyes was the semi-mythical forest

with the machinery at work, that had been sent out piecemeal from Turin. Here at work with missionaries and lay helpers were the blacks in the earliest stages of learning a trade; and with that, independence, self-fulfilment, in accordance with the Allamano method. Here were the farms and the coffee plantations, the most valuable resources for feeding the missions; but also the guarantee of a prosperous future, in Bishop Perlo's managerial vision.

Everything that passed before Camisassa's eyes ended up in his forty-four long letters to Turin. Including what he heard, as he listened to those who wanted to talk and those who did not care to. And then there was the checking of reports and letters from Turin, and comparing opinions and decisions against the actual facts. He was not, of course, entirely happy. And not merely because Bishop Perlo, inflexible in the first place with himself, had the kind of temperament he had, plus an absolute allergy to lay helpers, assistants, advisers: the fact of the matter was that the first missionaries had left Turin in very much of a hurry, since without a visible departure the Missionary Institute would have seemed to lack credibility. The pioneers' training had therefore had in part to be improvised; the capacities of each in the new surroundings, in relation to other missionaries and in contact with the local population had to be verified on the ground, there having been no means of testing it beforehand.

As well as the successes on which they could congratulate themselves (the catechists so much desired were there, were really there and the fruits of their labour should not be long to seek), Camisassa had also found problems, uncertainties, little personal misunderstandings, some to be straightened out with a kind word, others to be left to solve themselves. The assistant rector also encountered something like mistrust — or at least reluctance — in some, who were unwilling to open up to him, since he was the Vicar Apostolic's uncle. In brief, for better or worse, the inspection was truly indispensable after ten years of working under the standard of generous-hearted pioneering and the improvizations this had necessarily entailed. Giacomo Camisassa felt obliged to summon a sort of 'States General' for the voicing of congratulations, complaints and criticisms. There were many meetings with discussions

130

and bringing one another up to date, in the course of which a degree of tension was noticeable between Bishop Perlo and part of his personnel. The assistant rector had discovered many things, others however escaped him. All the same, he was able to prepare a decidedly rich, if not complete, body of experiences for Turin, to improve the systems of training in the Mother House and modify one or two ways of doing things too.

He had come to Africa with another task as well: to see on the spot what chances there were for missionary expansion. And on this point he was able to send Turin important information. He learned that the British authorities looked favourably on the setting up of Consolata mission stations in the Meru area, north-east of Mount Kenya. Forthwith Bishop Perlo set off to make a careful exploration of the sites, coming back with an entirely positive report: very promising natural surroundings, peaceful people. And this prompted the fifty-seven year old Canon Camisassa to leave in his turn for Meru. A journey totalling four hundred and fifty kilometres, partly on foot, partly by mule, at the end of which a report went off to the rector: 'The people are evidently related to the Akikuyu, since their language is almost identical; the people of Kiijà seem much simpler and better natured than the Akikuyu; those of Igogi more alert, robust and sturdy. [Kiijà, later becoming Imenti, and Egoji, were the places where Bishop Perlo had already planned to set up mission stations.] Our missionaries were received very cordially, much more so than in the early days by the Kikuyu.'

This was not enough. With his nephew, the bishop, he made further plans of a quite different type. One of them envisaged Consolata missions in the Upper Congo (now Zaire, in those days under Belgian sovereignty); and the other concerned the original and abiding dream of Giuseppe Allamano: to go to the Galla and take up Guglielmo Massaia's work among them once again. To go there, said uncle and nephew, not by a gradual and slow advance from Kenya, but by way of the Vatican. In other words, to get Propaganda Fide to assign the part of the Vicariate Apostolic of the Galla in Ethiopia, by erecting it into a Prefecture Apostolic: and this was the region of Southern Kafa, Galla territory.

Allamano for his part had never ceased to work in that direction. While Camisassa was in Africa, he happened to have to go to Rome for the cause of Don Cafasso's beatification; and there he took the opportunity of more than once seeing Cardinal Gotti, prefect of Propaganda Fide, finding him 'always affectionate and enthusiastic about us'. After these meetings he therefore wrote telling Camisassa to stop in Rome on his return journey, hurry to Propaganda Fide and immediately propose the matter of the new African prefecture.

Having disembarked at Naples on 19 April 1912, Giacomo Camisassa was already in Cardinal Gerolamo Antonio Gotti's presence the next day, with a map of the area spread out on the desk. It was obvious that in the very extensive Galla Vicariate, the French Capuchins with their Bishop Jarosseau could not be everywhere. Proceeding from this fact, the *iter* began that was to last for several months and load Allamano and Camisassa with work. It meant drawing up memorials, making accurate plans, taking on the work of map-making to show the boundaries of the territory very exactly. Meanwhile Propaganda Fide engaged in the ever bitter dialogue with Bishop Jarosseau, with a view to taking part of his territory away from him. (Also because this great missionary, who had been in Ethiopia for more than thirty years, had not completely renounced the evangelization of the Galla, despite the scarcity of personnel; rather, he was waiting for more peaceful times. Later, more than one sensational example of his apostolic vigour would be seen. He, André Jarosseau, would be the man to inaugurate the Catholic cathedral in Addis Ababa, and promote the training of Ethiopian priests in the seminary of the capital city. He eventually gave up his post, but certainly not for weariness on his part. The Italian occupation of Ethiopia forced him to leave.)

At last, while Pius X was actually considering Allamano's petition for a 'Mission Sunday' — in January 1913 — the decree was issued officially erecting the Prefecture Apostolic of Southern Kafa and entrusting it to the Consolata missionaries. The following May, the Prefect Apostolic was appointed: Fr Gaudenzio Barlassina who had joined Allamano's Institute ten years before. This man now having to make his debut in a front-line role was one of the rector's masterpieces and was to be among the successors of that master of priests and missionaries in the responsible position of Superior General.

The post that had just been assigned him was in one of the very few independent African states. Independent but shaken by recurrent convulsions, because of the difficulty in establishing a central power capable of imposing its authority on the *ras* of the various territories, and then of making it stick. In the nineteenth century the country had experienced a first relative awakening, due to a series of strong men, who made themselves emperor after subjugating the great feudatories. The first of these was *ras* Kassa, lord of the Shoa in 1856 and crowned emperor at Axum, but disastrously inept in foreign affairs; his high-handed treatment of British officials provoked a punitive expedition which encircled him in the fortress of Magdala, where he committed suicide in 1868. After some years of anarchy, the *ras* of Tigré proclaimed himself *negus negusti* (king of kings) with the name John IV; he also died in battle (1889) against the Mahdists or dervishes (who some years later were able to do battle with the Italians in Eritrea).

The Shoan *ras* Menelek then seized the empire, with the help of the Italian government with which he later signed the famous Treaty of Uccialli (1889). In it there was an article, Article 17, with discrepancies between the Italian and Amharic versions, owing to which the Crispi government believed that Menelek accepted an Italian protectorate, while the latter had not the slightest intention of doing so. There lay the root of the conflict that in March 1896 had led to the tragic defeat of the Italians at Adowa. Menelek founded the capital Addis Ababa and connected it by railway to the French coastal possession of Jibuti, a distance of more than seven hundred kilometres. He tried finally to ensure a peaceful succession to the throne by designating his nephew *lij* Yasu as his heir. The succession occurred in 1913 but three years later Yasu was excommunicated for his pro-Islamic sympathies. One of Menelek's daughters, Zauditù, then assumed the title of Empress, with *ras* Tafari Makonnen as Regent, later to become Emperor Haile Selassie.

The Christian history of Ethiopia is much longer. It

began in the fourth century with the landing of the Syrian merchant Frumentius on those coasts, who with his brother Aedesius was on his way home from India. Taken to the court, which in those days resided at Axum, they ended by joining and forming part of it. Frumentius in particular became treasurer of the kingdom and, after the sovereign's death, converted his widow to Christianity, thus founding a community of believers. Having left Ethiopia, he arrived in Alexandria, Egypt, where St Athanasius consecrated him bishop and persuaded him to go back to Ethiopia. Thus he became head of that Abyssinian Church which was later to be known as Coptic (Egyptian) for having, after the Council of Chalcedon, followed the Church of Alexandria into the monophysite heresy.

At the moment of his appointment, Fr Barlassina was in Kenya, and from there he came to Italy towards the end of 1913. Surprisingly, he was still there a year later. True, there were many things to be sorted out and got ready for the mission. There were also problems involving Italian politics, even involving a meeting between him and Camisassa in Rome with Ferdinando Martini, Minister for Colonies in the Salandra government. But the reason for the delay was really to be sought in Ethiopia, in the confused situation after Menelek's death and also in the political manoeuvring of the European powers. In a word, to *get* the Prefecture of Kafa had been something fairly simple. The big problem now was how to manage to get *into* it, and the solution took some waiting for.

10
'In pestilence, famine and war...'

At 2.30 in the afternoon of 28 June 1914, the Italian ministry for Foreign Affairs received Telegram No. 5730 from the Consulate in Sarajevo, Bosnia (part of the Austro-Hungarian Empire). It said: 'While driving to Town Hall, as result of bomb explosion, Crown Prince of Austria-Hungary and Princess have been killed.' Five hours later the same Consulate corrected: '... Princes' death due to revolver shots.' It was a Sunday, the vigil of the feast of Sts Peter and Paul. For this reason, as every year, towards evening Pope Pius X went down to pray at St Peter's tomb in the Vatican Basilica, and as he set off he said: 'Let us go and pray for the dead as well.' That is to say, for those two about whose deaths the Vatican had been informed by the Nuncio in Vienna. The first two victims of the First World War, Franz Ferdinand von Habsburg and his wife Sophia.

Then began the mad July of 1914. Between harsh demands, polemical replies, conciliatory proposals and hair-brained gestures, the machine for the destruction of Europe was set in motion. On 28 July, Austria-Hungary declared war on Serbia. And less than a month later, Germany, France, Great Britain, Russia, Belgium and remote Japan had all joined in the conflict.

Here then was the 'great war' that Pius X had feared. In an immediate appeal of his *Ad universos orbis catholicos*, he wrote: 'While almost all Europe has been swept into the abyss of a most disastrous war, the dangers, carnage and deadly consequences of which no one can contemplate without feeling crushed with grief and dread, we too cannot but be terribly afflicted by it and tormented by indescribable sadness of soul...' He fell sick with bronchitis, and the organism, already weakened by a previous illness

135

(nephritis with cardiac complications) was no longer strong enough to recover. During the night of 20 August, the life and pontificate of Pius X came to an end, while the war he had so much dreaded got into its stride. In the early days of September, the Genoese Giacomo Della Chiesa, Archbishop of Bologna, succeeded him as Benedict XV.

Italy declared herself to be neutral but had to prepare for any eventuality and hence began calling men to the colours. There was also a problem to be solved as to who should command the army; an unexpected vacancy had been left by the death of General Alberto Pollio in the Hotel Turin in Turin. General Luigi Cadorna took his place, while the controversy between interventionists and neutralists broke out. In October 1914, Cesare Battisti addressed the Turinese in Du Parc Restaurant.

The Consolata Missions however were already involved in the war. Hostility between Great Britain and Germany extended to their respective African colonies. Tanganyika, bordering on Kenya, was a German colony and had a military leader of exceptional talent, Colonel Paul von Lettow-Vorbeck. Encircled by enemies, he with a very bold guerrilla strategy was to resist for four years, only capitulating in 1918 on orders from Berlin. Hence Bishop Perlo's Vicariate got caught up in the problems of war, while maritime communication with Italy became increasingly difficult and one consignment of stores was to be lost, due to the sinking of the ship.

On 28 December 1914, Gaudenzio Barlassina, the new Prefect Apostolic of Kafa, left for Africa with two priests, two brothers and four sisters, among whom was Irene Stefani who had her own very special 'appointment' with the war in Africa. At one time they were afraid the Suez Canal might be closed, which would have cut the connections between the missionaries and Turin.

Joseph Allamano, like so many others, felt that Italy's hour too was approaching. Italy had already received a colossal blow in January 1915 with the Marsica earthquake: thirty thousand dead, many thousands of bewildered orphans. (Fr Luigi Orione was making these his concern, just as he had heroically done in the earthquake at Messina; and that time he had asked Canon Allamano for a picture of the

Consolata to go in one of the first of the chapels improvized after the disaster.)

'A great earthquake! What a calamity! More than thirty thousand people killed. . . And then there's the war! It's devastating! We must pray. . .' Now there was a continual echo of these events in the rector's talks. One of the brothers had already been called up. Italy was proceeding towards the so-called 'red mobilization', devised by Cadorna to put the country quietly on a war footing, since he was negotiating intervention against Austria. Mobilizations, armies, wars, were all things of a different world for the native gentleness of Joseph Allamano, who was in an immediate position to gauge the practical effects these had on family life. 'How wretched, how sad it is!' he confided to his circle. 'Especially for the mothers and wives, coming to the Consolata to commend themselves to the Lord, and no one knows where we are going to end up. . . A man from Brandizzo told me: "I had two sons and they've taken them away, I had three head of cattle and they've taken two of them." '

At times, he expresses discouragement; like others, he speaks of 'God's punishment'. But what he was actually doing meanwhile was more than courageous; to some people it looked absolute folly. For, having sold the buildings in Corso Duca di Genova, he began work in April 1915 on extending the Mother House with a view to admitting one hundred sisters.

On 24 May Italy entered the war and the call-up emptied the Missionary Institute. Once war had been declared, there was no further exemption for men within the national frontiers. In a short time, thirty-eight of the priests and brothers were in uniform. For the remainder — the not-so-young men and the sisters — it was also now a matter of making sacrifices over food, and of facing up to winters with little or no heating.

And so it was to go on till the end of the war, with the public scourges that invariably come together: war was attended by famine, later followed by the fearful epidemic called 'Spanish flu', killing off thousands, and restoring meaning to the ancient, cumulative petition: '*A peste, fame et bello, libera nos, Domine*' ('From plague, famine and war, deliver us, O Lord'). The rector did his best to look after those who remained behind, meanwhile most assiduously following the progress of those who were serving with the armed forces; he wrote regularly to all of these, either personally or with the help of Fr Umberto Costa; he also sent them all a monthly report on the life of the Institute, which was called *Da Casa Madre* (*From Mother House*).

A new wing of the House, the one for the Sisters, was barely completed, in February 1917, when the military authorities requisitioned it for use as a depot for medical stores. The same Mother House was shortly afterwards to be partially taken over for barracks. There was one cheerful interlude among these problems: the beatification of Joseph Benedict Cottolengo, celebrated in Rome on 16 April. The Consolata Institute solemnized the event by making a collective pilgrimage to his tomb in the Little House. But, shortly afterwards, new blows. On 11 June, the theology student Eugenio Baldi died in action on the Vodice, and in August the notorious 'Turin riots' occurred.

The exceptionally cold winter of 1916–1917 was followed by a dramatic spring: rise in the cost of living, disorganization of food supplies and periodic disappearance of bread from the city's shops. The war had meanwhile entered its third year without any convincing sign of an approaching peace: there were the usual announcements, usual bulletins, usual massacres on the Isonzo Valley over a kilometre or two of land. In the spontaneous demonstrations that occurred in the city's working-class quarters, protests over the cost of living merged with hostility to the war, even more so once the thrilling news arrived about the revolution in Russia: the one in March that put an end to Tzarism. In Petrograd too it had all begun with demonstrations about bread. In August, then, a delegation of Russian revolutionaries arrived in Turin (the Mensheviks; the Bolsheviks had not yet come to power); and this rapid move gave rise to heated demonstrations of much more radical temper than before.

A few days later (21 August) while this atmosphere persisted, Turin found itself virtually without bread. This time, it was no longer demonstrations, but revolt, which began with the peaceful sending of a delegation to City Hall and then exploded in barricades, attacks on and looting of shops and finally in brutal assaults on some of the churches: arson, pillage, profanation, vandalism, particularly at the Church of San Bernardino, but also the Churches of Our Lady of Peace and of Our Lady of Health. From the parish priest of Our lady of Peace, Mgr Michele Mossotto, who was seventy-one, the rioters took everything including the ciboriums out of the tabernacles. Canon Allamano immediately sent him a gift of money. Mossotto took it, thanked the bearer, then returned it: 'Give it to Canon Allamano as my contribution to the missions. Providence will look after me.'

In the city, troops intervened and clashes went on until the evening of Saturday, 25 August. After which the dead were counted and about fifty people were said to have lost their lives, including three soldiers; but no really accurate figure could be known. At the Consolata there were only a few broken panes of glass, since the Shrine had been under guard. The rector announced special prayers and referred to the events in his spiritual talks. And this attack on the churches must have affected him deeply, especially because at that very time everyone was discussing Benedict XV's peace initiative, with his celebrated Peace Note on the 'futile slaughter', and almost the entire official and governmental world (with Italy in the lead) was attacking the Pope and his invitations to a peace without reparations or spoils of war. In a word, from 'the Right', attacks on the Pontiff; from 'the Left', the burning of churches. . .

How do we get into Ethiopia?

But for Canon Allamano, Giacomo Camisassa and the whole Institute, the war was not exclusively in Europe. There was Africa. The activities of Bishop Perlo and his people in Kenya had to be supported; the effective creation of the Prefecture Apostolic of Kafa had to be followed up. And here there began a sort of intrigue, intra-Ethiopian on the one hand, British-French-Italian on the other, with Propaganda Fide for good measure; and the whole thing provoked an incredible postal and telegraphic traffic between European capitals, ports on the African coast and villages up-country, with a series of scene changes hard to follow.

We have already seen that, after being appointed, the new Prefect Apostolic, Fr Gaudenzio Barlassina stayed on in Italy for a long while, until December 1914. And the delay before he could really settle into his job was also to be very long, for the following reason: Propaganda Fide had traced the boundaries of a certain territory on a map and given it the ecclesiastical title of 'Prefecture of Kafa' and assigned the task of preaching the Catholic faith there to the Consolata missionaries. But the territory formed part of the Ethiopian empire, so before one could enter it and work there, permission was needed from the Ethiopian authorities. But, at that moment — between Menelek's death and the short-lived succession, until the regency of *ras* Tafari Makonnen (the future Haile Selassie) who had not as yet imposed his authority on all the *ras* of the various territories — they worked in the realm of theory only. The French government, through its representatives, sided with Bishop Jarosseau's Capuchins (who were French), to influence the native rulers in turn through them; and indeed *ras* Tafari did take a lot of notice of advice from Bishop Jarosseau, who normally resided in Harar. The Italian government for its part was keen to see an Italian missionary presence in Ethiopia for similar reasons (but also because some of its representatives on the spot knew the Consolata Institute and held it in high esteem). Everyone however had to bear in mind that *ras* Tafari, aspiring to total power over all Ethiopia, for the time being depended on the support of the senior Coptic clergy, who were hardly well-disposed towards the white missionaries. The British government for its part was keenly interested in a missionary penetration from the south, that is to say, from the territory forming Bishop Perlo's Vicariate Apostolic.

From Turin, the most complicated gymkhana had to be followed: of proposals, initiatives, agreements, disagreements, permits and prohibitions, all involving Propaganda Fide too. Multilateral negotiations lasting as long as the whole First World War. Longer still in fact, beyond the end of hostilities and the peace treaties.

To simplify the matter, here are the significant moments

of the affair. Since the original objective had been to reach the Galla in Kafa from the south, that is to say, from Kenya, a first attempt was made even before Fr Barlassina arrived in Africa.

On 21 November 1914, an expedition left Nyeri with Fr Angelo Dal Canton and Bros Aquilino Caneparo and Anselmo Jeantet. These first reached Moyale, a British post on the border with Ethiopia, staying there for almost the whole of April 1915 (by which time Fr Barlassina had arrived in Kenya). They then entered Ethiopian territory and halted at Burji, six hundred kilometres away from their destination. Not only this: they still needed permission from the Ethiopian authorities. They gave themselves out to be merchants and were eventually granted a *laissez-passer*, but this was for Addis Ababa, not for Kafa. So they stayed put in Burji, and there they were arrested as false merchants (having no merchandise). They were imprisoned for almost two months; conditions were not cruel and Fr Dal Canton was even able to send messages off to Joseph Allamano. It did however mean that the operation had failed. Released in August, the 'merchants' had to go back to Kenya.

Meanwhile another operation had become intertwined with this one. Or perhaps it was little more than a day-dream. Bishop Perlo on the one part and Italian officials on the other thought of entering Ethiopia in the guise of a duly constituted commercial company: something quite legal, which the Italian government could therefore legally support. These proceedings did not inspire Joseph Allamano with any enthusiasm; in his view, the priests and brothers of the Consolata ought to go about the world 'with head held high, like missionaries'. And, furthermore, the Holy See had issued clear and over-all prohibitions against schemes of this sort, so Propaganda Fide vetoed the commercial company. Meanwhile, the most unexpected, most illegal yet evangelical thing had occurred: Fr Barlassina had entered Ethiopia on his own and was already in Addis Ababa.

How had he done it? To start with, he had gone a different way; instead of entering Ethiopia from the south, he left Kenya for Mogadishu, went on to Aden and from there to Jibuti, where he caught the train. Having covered some distance by rail, he proceeded by other means. And on

Christmas night 1916 he entered Addis Ababa clandestinely on a mule and took a room in a hotel. All completely illegal. His mandate as Prefect Apostolic had no force in Ethiopian eyes. More alone than this he could not be.

At just about the same time, the drama — and humanly speaking the failure — of another man alone in Africa came to an end. Charles de Foucauld in Algeria had founded (or dreamed of founding?) a new religious congregation, that of the Little Brothers of Jesus; and he was its only member when he was murdered at Tamanrasset in 1916. Once he was buried, the second Little Brother arrived, and others after him.

Gaudenzio Barlassina knew nothing of this, for Charles de Foucauld died in obscurity. All the same, he was prepared for many surprises in his experience of Africa. Illegal immigrant as he was, he went about like a member of the middle class, he did not preach, he did not perform acts of worship in public, but meanwhile he tried to make friends, people who would support him and initially give a legal connotation to his presence on Ethiopian soil. That was the first point. The second was to be the recognition of his Prefecture. But this took time. The mission would have to wait: the boredom of seeing days and years go by with nothing decided. In Turin, Allamano had trained him for this too, with his teaching so firmly opposed to the unrealistic approach. (To Fr Sales, that effective promoter of missionary vocations, the rector recommended a sober approach in his recruiting talks: 'Because I know that in that seminary there will be people who want to learn about our Institute, with prudence and the superiors' approval, you may speak about it. But be careful not to be over-enthusiastic. Tell them what the Institute is really like: about the discipline and the spirit that rules it.')

Buttonholing certain authorities through Italian intermediaries, he managed to get a residence permit for the districts of Leka and Challa which were both in the Prefecture. This was an important step, since he was allowed to go there without paying any special political or commercial tolls. Sure, he was not allowed to preach. He remained a member of the middle class. Yet he was actually there and had no need of cover, of appealing to legations on the spot and ministries in some capital. He also received letters from Turin and from Bishop Perlo, 'who advanced the same argument but without the same conclusion.' Joseph Allamano and Filippo Perlo saw things in different lights. And he on the spot had to adapt himself to situations by finding his own solutions step by step and abandoning, if need be, his priestly garb, because the important thing was not to sow alarm and not to get himself expelled. Just as Our Lord behaved, in his own time, who 'besides not wearing distinctive clothes which might have caused alarm, got into a boat for some apparent purpose, only to manifest himself when the time was ripe; he certainly had not been invited to give a sermon by the Pharisee in whose house he met Mary Magdalen.' This was what he wrote to Bishop Perlo, ever in contact with the Italian government through that commercial company which in the end did not work: political conditions having changed, whereas the Barlassina way of doing things step by step worked very well. In 1919 he had six missionaries with him in the Kafa Prefecture. Guglielmo Massaia's work among the Galla could begin again.

The war in Africa

Antonio Cavicchioni, Italian Consul in Nairobi, wrote in April 1916 to Ferdinando Martini, Minister for Colonies, telling him of the appalling death rate among the negro carriers. Having to fight the Germans of neighbouring Tanganyika, the British had enlisted one lot of negroes into military units and the others as carriers. The latter numbered some six thousand men and played a very important role, for they assured the supply of provisions and munitions from the ports to the front lines, which at one point extended into Tanganyika. They carried the loads on their shoulders, in a territory with hardly any roads; a hard and continuous work to which their physiques were unaccustomed and through unhealthy terrains very different from the verdant Kikuyu. The result was physical deterioration, malaria, dysentery, various forms of exhaustion and insanity. Consul Cavicchioni wrote: 'From a rough estimate it would seem that only 25% of those thus impressed will

143

return in good health to their villages. The rest will be either dead or disabled.'

The British command was consequently obliged to set up a series of hospitals for these people. They were sited at Mombasa, Nairobi, Voi and later also at Kisumu, Kisii, Taveta. . .

They were badly off for doctors, but worse still for nurses: few and incompetent, few and lazy. Then from the Kikuyu lands, Bishop Perlo sent down the greater part of his missionaries and sisters to these hospitals. There were two groups of sisters: the Vincentians from the Cottolengo, who had not yet been repatriated, and the Consolata ones. The former, helped in this situation by their specialist training, intervened with prompt efficiency; but, to call these places hospitals was completely misleading. Some of them were more like a gathering of dozens and dozens of Jobs 'sitting in ashes, one malignant sore from the soles of their feet to the top of their head', lacking even the strength to scratch themselves with a potsherd. Here is a description of a 'ward' in the hospital at Voi: 'About eighty men, half-naked, gaunt, dishevelled, with sad, haunted eyes in unrecognizable faces, lay hugger-mugger on camp beds or reed matting, while others were squashed up together on a huge communal bed of dry grass in one corner of the ward. One bewildering combination of moaning, raving and cursing in a babel of incomprehensible languages, in a nightmarish atmosphere and unbearable stench.'

Such was the vision appearing before the eyes of one of the Consolata Sisters, Irene Stefani of Brescia, aged twenty-five, who had been in Africa since 1915: 'The moment I crossed the threshold, the scene presented to my eyes was so unexpected that I had to step back, vomiting with nausea and horror.' Gian Paola Mina recreates the scene in her biography and describes Sr Irene's effort to conquer her repugnance and get used to it: 'With a supreme effort of will, with clenched teeth, she re-entered the ward and went up to a young man who was foaming at the mouth and had eyes full of pus. She cleaned him up, helped him to sit up in his bunk; he was burning with fever. One of the so-called male nurses had left some water nearby and gone away. "Are you thirsty?" she asked him, raising the bowl to

144

his parched lips. He made no reply but greedily drank a few gulps. Sr Irene talked to him for a little while, then tried to approach another sick man: again she was assailed by nausea and had to rush out into the sun and air. . .'

In East Africa, the First World War ended five days later than in Europe, since the indomitable Lettow-Vorbeck, having moved from Tanganyika into Portuguese Mozambique and then into the British possessions of Nyassaland and Rhodesia, only laid down his arms on receipt of peremptory orders from Germany. In Nairobi, the Allied victory was celebrated with the roll of drums, brass bands, parades, flags flying and the awarding of medals. As well as the officers and soldiers, the missionaries were also given decorations, as were the sisters too, who had expected anything to happen in the mission field except being made Commanders of the British Empire at the hand of an Anglican Governor in a scarlet tunic.

Young Sr Irene and her fellow-sisters received two commemorative medals. She had learnt by now not to break down at anything. The war no doubt left her with memories of many a feverish, staring, rolling eye of men sunk in the last degree of helplessness, and of those same eyes brought back to serenity by the smile, by the care and the courage of her twenty-five years: eyes of so many men whose language she did not know and to whom she had only known how to say the minimal essentials between one spoonful of broth and the next, between a sip of water and medical treatment. On a certain day, thousands of worn-out men, at a certain gesture of Sr Irene's, began recovering their human dignity, recovering hope: some for as many years as their lives lasted, others for a few days or a few hours. She also catechized them, with measured and essential talks in the local language learnt with great difficulty, and corroborated by her conduct of every day and moment in a 'language' everyone could understand. Many joyfully accepted her suggestion that they should be baptized, and took a new name which was often Giovanni, the name of Irene's father. Thus an African Christianity began to grow in the zone behind the front amid dysentery and malaria. Referring to these converts in her letters, Sr Irene spoke of their 'Souls' with a capital letter, as if bowing her head each time before

145

the immortal creature each one of them was. In her simplified way, she a Brescian innkeeper's daughter, was a good theologian.

She had learnt her 'theology' in Via della Circonvallazione in Turin, from the talks and conversations with the rector, with that quiet voice of his that never asserted itself and yet left such a deep impression. As Joseph Allamano had striven to build this sister and many another, so we can glimpse from her letters written to him how all missionaries ought to behave. Here is one of February 1918 addressed, as all her others were, to the 'most venerated and beloved Father.' First of all, she thanks him 'for everything you have done and are still doing for me.' Then she goes on to describe the first missionary phase at Nyeri: 'My job was to help prune the coffee bushes; I liked this very much. . . My work mate was the kind and experienced Sr Costanza. . . I stayed at Nyeri for about seventeen months. From there obedience sent me to help out in the wartime African hospitals.' She goes on to speak of the varying ways in which the sick reacted to her religious suggestions: '. . . others however did not want to know and of these last a good many came my way. So many that at times I thought those *dark hours* had arrived, which you, most venerated Father, predicted to me back home! I remembered your teachings, I followed the example of Sr Cristina by uniting one or two *little sacrifices*.' This was what she called the struggle not to break down when faced with such repugnant situations, and the courage to go back 'inside' after the bouts of vomiting.

In difficult moments, the letter goes on, she and Sr Cristina consulted one of the missionaries, Fr Panelatti: 'We must always remember that our most venerated Father Founder in Turin is a true missionary to the entire world and not merely to Africa. Let us unite our intentions and works to his intense and effective work and we shall find a potent aid.' Good results came of it; the letter goes on: 'Then, following this great victory, after a *Deo gratias* to Heaven, our spontaneous, most lively and heartfelt thanks went ever out to you, Most Venerated Father, who in your fatherly love are helping us all the time even though we are so far away.'

Here Joseph Allamano's missionary teaching is seen, not

in its methodical unwinding day by day but in one of its results. One of the very many, whether he was near or far away, whether he was alive or dead. 'I want you to be manly and supple,' his quiet voice used to tell the sisters. So it was with Sr Irene and with all the Consolata Missionary Sisters who have now adopted it as one of their mottos.

Sr Irene died on the eve of All Saints 1930, after sixteen years in the missions, at Gikondi. In her last hours, the witnesses questioned by Gian Paola Mina reported, she was delirious. But it was a 'missionary's delirium'. For, speaking in Kikuyu as though she were among her blacks, she kept repeating: 'God is good and everyone should believe in his envoy, the Lord Jesus Christ. Redemption lies in that name and in being baptized in the name of the Father and of the Son and of the Holy Spirit. . .' Thus the Servant of God, Sr Irene Stefani, for whose beatification the canonical process is now in motion, bore witness for Joseph Allamano, that trainer of parish priests who had never himself been a parish priest, that moulder of men and women for modern missionary work, who had never set foot outside Italy.

'I think about these things on my way back and forth to the cathedral,' he told his people in Mother House. He went to the cathedral, as we know, to sing the Divine Office which was his duty as a canon. And thus, going along, 'these things' occupied his mind. He noted them down as soon as he got home and they then formed the material for his talks, some of them on the long side, embellished with apparent digressions about incidents and memories of long ago. By means of these discourses delivered *en famille* he injected into their bloodstream such limpid concepts, such hard-headed, far-sighted warnings, as no one could ever forget and which would therefore spring suddenly to mind at the appropriate moment, as with Sr Irene. The rector's gentle voice could on occasion grow harsh in rebutting the lies current about missionaries; as for instance the saying that all they needed was 'half an education and second class talents; which is equivalent to demeaning the holiest and highest of vocations to the level of any old career, open as a refuge and escape for any imbecile. No! the apostolate in our day, more than ever before, needs people first class in virtue and doctrine.'

That was why, in the hospitals of Africa, Fr Panelatti could say that the mild and reserved priest in Turin was a missionary 'to the entire world': Joseph Allamano, the man of the modern mission field, with the extraordinary ability to see and to some extent live the situations and problems without moving off his home ground; going from Consolata to cathedral, from Consolata to Mother House, from confessional to retreats. And those who come to him ill-prepared or, worse still, deluded, will soon have their eyes opened soberly, honestly, briskly for them. 'For those who beguile themselves with transient fancies, by half-desires that today are fire and tomorrow are nothing, for the apathetic who do not perhaps give dissatisfaction to their superiors but no consolation either, for the whimperers who have always got some little thing wrong with them and never let up, for the faint-hearted and the slackers, for the everlasting malcontents and the incorrigible gossips: for all these there is no possibility of serious training in Mother House, no hope of useful activity in the mission field. For them therefore the main gates are open if they are still novices; and if they are already professed, relegation to some corner as a nuisance.'

Sometimes however he seemed subject to implacable fixations, notwithstanding his sweetness of temperament and that 'beautiful smile' of which one of his pupils, Fr Alessandro Cantono of the Pastoral Institute, speaks. Over foreign languages, for instance, he would allow no respite for anyone, especially in English. He wanted what today we call total immersion, not considering the hours of lessons and practical exercise sufficient; so he orders daily conversation periods, even on holidays. And even the recreational small-talk after supper had to be conducted in English. Lastly, on Sunday, the seminarians turn by turn would have to explain the epistle of the day in English, — with him always present, who did not understand a word but would not go away.

11
The bitterest blow

'Those who want beards, raise your hands!' All were raised but one, and Joseph Allamano then proclaimed freedom of beard in the Consolata Missionary Institute: 'Away with razors!' He did not wear one; he never was to grow one; he would never do anything which to the slightest external detail might seem to alter his quality or appearance as a priest of the Diocese of Turin. But he had to give these lads a little satisfaction: among them were some who had come back from the war, and all were training for the missions, where a beard was almost *de rigueur*. Let the ones here in Mother House feel a bit nearer, at least in this, to those who are already on the African front line. At least in this: for the rest, however, Joseph Allamano did not modify or edulcorate the seriousness of the training one jot.

If on 1 July 1919, he accepted the vote about beards; the following July he spoke very clearly to everybody: 'There is an urge among the priests and theology students who have come back from the forces to rush their studies for ordination and the sacred ministry. I sympathize; for them, that was time as good as wasted, since they were able to study little or nothing. It was a misfortune, like an illness. . . That however does not make it right to skip what is needful for one's studies, worse still for piety and virtue. . . Away with this urge to rush things. The Church is not in such desperate need of subjects. . . She can continue her mission without them; what she does need are learned ministers, well trained in spirit. . . No one is necessary to the Church, but well trained and learned ministers are useful.'

On that first day of June 1919, a small celebration took place at Mother House: prayers and hymns before a picture of the Consolata, and then a bonfire of all the letters priests, theology students and brothers serving in the forces had written to the rector during the war. All burnt, as though to cancel all those sorry memories and everyone's sufferings (the *sagrin*, as the rector said in Piedmontese).

Sorrow and suffering that had also afflicted those who stayed at home. The epidemic of the Spanish flu caused casualties like a war, throughout Europe and even in the United States. At certain periods of 1918, the number of people who died in Turin of the Spanish flu rose to one hundred a day. It was a new disease: prevention was almost impossible, apart from the usual and disregarded advice to cover one's nose and mouth with a gauze mask. In October 1918, the elementary and intermediate schools did not reopen, and for a short while the authorities closed down places of entertainment too. All this until the beginning of 1919, when the disease began losing its virulence. The religious communities of Turin were badly hit. At the Consolata Institute, one of the students died. The Spanish flu then killed Bro Giacomo Gaidano in Nyeri.

Fr Umberto Costa was however carried off by another illness in January 1918 at the age of only thirty-two; he was the first of the rector's young assistants and, among other things, had with him conducted the correspondence with their fellow-members while on active service. Joseph Allamano had thought of entrusting him with the running of Mother House; now, for this purpose, he recalled Fr Tommaso Gays from Africa. No sooner was one problem solved than new ones arose.

There was also a very sad case of desertion: a priest. Allamano had already got him released from military service; on being discharged, he first wanted to leave the Institute, no longer feeling called to be a missionary. Finally he left the priesthood as well.

(There were also problems at the Pastoral Institute. Here, in 1916, the call-up had left the place almost empty. And this being so, the spiritual director Fr Luigi Boccardo decided to resign after thirty years in harness. His brother, Fr Giovanni Maria having died at Pancalieri, he went and succeeded him as director of the Daughters of San Gaetano. In 1919, the Pastoral Institute having come back to life, the spiritual direction was entrusted to Fr Gabriele Lorenzatti.)

Once the rooms and halls of Mother House had been vacated, regular academic years could begin again. As a result of the relationship between Joseph Allamano and Cardinal Willem van Rossum, the new Prefect of the Congregation of Propaganda Fide, eight priests, five brothers, fifty-four seminarians, plus twenty-two boys of the Minor Seminary, were admitted to the Turin headquarters. In the Kenya mission with Bishop Perlo there were thirty-one priests, thirteen brothers and nineteen Consolata Missionary Sisters, plus thirty-six Vincentian Sisters from the Cottolengo. With Fr Barlassina in the Prefecture Apostolic of Kafa, there were four priests and two brothers.

At the beginning of 1919, U.S. President Wilson was feted with exceptional warmth in Turin as everywhere else in Europe. He was regarded as being mainly responsible for the peace and there were triumphal celebrations wherever he appeared. Even his brief halt in Turin ended with a lunch in the Philarmonica. At that moment the name of Wilson brought almost everyone into agreement. But the reasons for agreement were not to be found in this feverish post-war period: feverish not only owing to Spanish flu. We have reached the times of economic convulsion, with factories closing, unemployment, rising inflation and the disillusioned, demobilized masses, the bitterness of feeling one did not count, the wish to make others pay in every sort of way. . . Then, there is the example of Russia: Lenin with his Bolsheviks in power, the birth of a state 'of workers and peasants', heralding revolution for the whole western world.

These were days and months of drama and tragedy, often with people being killed and wounded on the streets of Turin, with arson and destruction of a different type from that of 1917. It is interesting to see how this was known and felt in the little world of the Missionary Institute. Though the fires were sometimes started by fascist gangs, the flames reminded priests, sisters and seminarians of those that burned down San Bernardino's. Only, this time, the movement seemed on a much vaster scale, destined to last and — who could tell? — get much worse. So one of the sisters asked the rector: 'Suppose there were to be a persecution, Father?' This was what people were thinking, yet Allamano saw things in a totally different light, as his reply outlines the grim scenario: 'Suppose there were to be a persecution? Well, if there were, those of us at the Shrine would take care to remove the Blessed Sacrament and then the image of the Consolata. . . We shall take position before the altar and if they want to take the Blessed Sacrament, they will have to shoot us, kill us first; and then we shall be martyrs for the Blessed Sacrament. And you, down here, will do the same. . . Oh yes, yes, these are bad times to be sure; but this does not stop us from becoming saints.'

The last phrase is the one that should command attention: for Joseph Allamano, bad times were never an alibi or an obstacle. He deplored them bitterly, but he knew how to get round them. There was something about him that reminds us a little of the early days of the pontificate of Gregory the Great, when Rome was besieged by Agilulf's Lombards and Italy was afflicted with famine and plague. Gregory's sermons at the time were all predictions of catastrophe, urging Christians to do penance in expectation of Judgement Day; at the same time, however, his actions were impassioned reactions to every disaster, characterized by the most trusting and optimistic efficiency. In his Turinese and African (and even Roman) dimensions, Joseph Allamano too behaved somewhat in this two-handed way. He electrifies the sisters with a vision of sacrifice at the altar steps, descants too on the sadness of the times and the moral degradation that is its cause. At the same time, however, he goes on fighting with his usual spirit — and Camisassa with him — on the usual fronts.

The beatification of Joseph Cafasso (how many years had he been concerned with this?) was reaching its final lap. In the spring of 1919, the examination concerning miracles being finished in Turin, he himself took the documents to Rome. And on that occasion was received in audience by Pope Benedict XV. In February 1921 he went back to Rome again for the last and decisive run-up to the finishing post: the reading of the decree on the heroic virtues of the Servant of God, in the presence of the Pope. The last and decisive run-up did not however mean that beatification was near, as Allamano was to have reason to discover. Still, he was grateful to Benedict XV for his interest in the cause; besides, of course, for the great missionary Encyclical

Maximum Illud, stimulating many organizations to support the missions; and for intervening wisely and forcefully to deplore the petty jealousies between one religious family and another in the mission field.

This time they were not to meet again, for Benedict XV died on 22 January 1922, even before the three 'ante-preparatory congregations' which began the final lap of the procedure for Cafasso. The 'congregations' were nonetheless to be held at the established times, during the pontificate of Pius XI. Eventually Allamano in Turin received the news he had been waiting for a lifetime: the beatification was certain, absolutely certain; but not immediately. It was fixed for 1925.

Another of his battle fronts was of course Africa, with an unexpected new ingredient. Originally it had been he, Joseph Allamano, who had gone in search of territories to evangelize. Now, instead, they were being offered to him, and he accepted them from a sense of obedience, short as he was of personnel and material resources. The place in question was Iringa, a territory 'as large as Piedmont and half Lombardy', actually belonging to Tanganyika, the former German colony. It was now a British mandate; the German missionaries had quit the field and the Consolata Institute filled the void. Bishop Perlo sent one or two missionaries from Kenya and others arrived from Turin. Between here and Rome, the most pedantic negotiations then took place over the borders, after which, in March 1920, the Prefecture Apostolic of Iringa came into existence, with Giuseppe Allamano's Institute appointed to run it. On the list of names submitted for consideration, Propaganda Fide chose the first, to be Prefect: Fr Francesco Cagliero, born at Castelnuovo.

The rector's seventieth birthday had come and gone and he was getting a little weary of advising, proposing, pleading and negotiating, while still doing all his normal jobs and other sometimes quite disagreeable: as for instance disputes with other religious families in Africa, and in Italy too. In Italy, in fact, a controversy had been dragging on for years with the Congregation of the Virgin Mary about rights over the Shrine of the Consolata, involving not only the Archbishop but also the Holy See. And the rector for his part would not live to see the end of it.

He was anxious now to see the status of his own family, the Consolata Missionary Institute, settled, for there had been no advance, juridically speaking, since 1909 and the *Decretum laudis*. That is to say, he had received the Holy See's invitation to proceed with the matter, a preliminary encouragement. The decisive act for its future however lay in the approval of the Constitutions, on the basis of which the Institute would then become self-governing. So from 1909 until 1921, the Holy See had nominated and confirmed (for two consecutive six-year periods) Allamano as rector and Camisassa as vice rector; the Institute thus existing all this time on a provisional system of government, one of expectancy. The war was to blame too, of course. But now the time had come to put matters in order.

Allamano foresaw the convocation of the General Chapter for 1921 (when the second six-year period expired): the fundamental, creative moment which was to give the Institute its permanent organs of government. With this in mind, he had sent a new draft of the Constitutions to Rome, amended in accordance with suggestions from those priests of the Institute whom he had consulted. Propaganda Fide however took the opposite view: first hold the meeting of the chapter to revise the Constitutions, which should be submitted to Rome *after* being approved by the Chapter Fathers. In a word, until 1921 there was nothing more to be done, and the rector and assistant rector had to remain at their posts, 'protagonists', until the Chapter was held.

Allamano and Camisassa did not want to attend it. Not because they did not love the Institute; on the contrary: they wanted to see it finally established and recognized, with its own heads and its own rules, with a clearly defined and certain future, and so that the two of them could go back to being what they always and most deeply were: two priests of the diocese of Turin who, *as such*, had done missionary work, this being the normal institutional duty of any diocese, of any particular Church and of each of its priests.

Certainly Allamano would then have been spared a number of disappointments. But these fell to his lot, and not a few. We have already seen one of his most remarkable intuitions at work: that of requiring his people to confide in him completely by means of the diaries each of them was required to send him. It was all these sheets of paper that made it possible for him to be present in Kenya, in Tanganyika and in Ethiopia, among the missionaries, lay brothers and sisters, to understand what was said and what was unsaid, to intervene at times concerning others and even concerning himself. Well, these very diaries and letters had shown him there were bitter aspects to life in the mission field, the pettinesses of men and women who at other moments knew how to be great. . . And all those who unburdened their hearts to him were certain of a reply: fatherly, severe when necessary, but always absolutely honest and humane in what he demanded, open-hearted in his help. He had saved and reconstructed so many of them from his writing desk at the Consolata, but he had not been able to resolve all problems. There was a grave one, turning up in many a letter from Africa and in many a conversation in Turin: Bishop Filippo Perlo.

There was no doubt about it: this man had been a formidable discovery of Joseph Allamano's and Giacomo Camisassa's, for taking the first steps in Africa, for doing battle with so many different coalitions of interest for the sake of the Christian faith. Filippo Perlo was extraordinarily intelligent and strong-willed, no situation found him at a loss, no one could outdo him either in energy or in consistency, for what he demanded of others he first required of himself. And that was the point. Not all were like him. The most special wisdom is needed to detect each individual's potentials and limits, so as to apportion the weights and assign the day's march. But not everyone has this, and Filippo Perlo certainly did not, wanting everyone to be cast in the same metal as himself. His behaviour, many people also complained, was not fatherly. He was more like a general than a bishop. He was an autocrat. He was 'an autocratic general', one priest wrote.

In the main, Allamano thought these criticisms somewhat exaggerated, attributing them, in part at least, to the objective difficulties of living and living together in African situations. But the voices virtually grew into a chorus. And at length came that bitter period of Bishop Perlo's stay in Italy from April to November 1921.

He was Vicar Apostolic and a Bishop, and as such,

in Turin, was given a solemn reception and a room opposite the rector's at the Shrine of the Consolata. It could have been a non-stop party: the founder and the Institute's first Bishop, the vice rector's nephew for good measure. . . Instead they were bitter months. According to Fr Luigi Massa: 'When Bishop Perlo came to Italy in 1921, relations between him and the founder can be deduced from this fact. One morning Fr Manfredi was in the office with the founder, when the man-servant came in with a note from Bishop Perlo. Allamano read it, then with a sigh exclaimed: ''You see, Bishop Perlo and I no longer get on together; we communicate by means of little notes.'' Note that Bishop Perlo had the room opposite Allamano's; there was only the width of the corridor between them.'

They certainly did not understand each other. Divergent views on missionary work, temperamental differences. The fact of the matter was that things reached painful and insulting extremes. Having done all he had to do in Italy, Bishop Perlo left without even taking leave of the founder. Not a word. And the founder then went to Porta Nuova Station to say goodbye — almost furtively — at least to Bro Davide Balbiano, who was travelling with the Bishop. Balbiano later described what happened: 'He climbed into the carriage, gave me a few words of advice, presented me with a small edition of the *Imitation of Christ*, blessed me and said goodbye. Then he got out of the carriage, all huddled up and without a glance at anyone, and he went away very dejected and grieved about what had happened.'

The book of the *Imitation*, his invariable present to friends, the daily provender of his 'ruminating'! He must certainly have known by heart the little page devoted to the faults of others: 'Whatever a man is unable to correct in himself or in others, he should bear patiently until God ordains otherwise. Consider, it is perhaps better thus, for the testing of our patience. . . Whenever such obstacles confront you, pray to God that he may grant you his help, and give you grace to endure them in good heart. If anyone who has been once or twice warned remains obdurate, do not argue with him, but commit all things to God, that his will may be done. . .' (I, 16, 1).

Joseph Allamano must have wondered an infinity of

times: why did Filippo Perlo resemble his uncle Giacomo Camisassa in so many of his gifts, yet not in humility? Was there not leader material, the stuff great leaders are made of, in the assistant rector too, accustomed as he was 'to being top in everything' as his school-fellows used to say? Camisassa had overcome every test, while he was studying, when he was teaching, as the organizer of expeditions, workshops and building sites, subtle doctor in the most complex curial questions, tough antagonist of the most ruthless businessmen, affectionate adviser to the poor who came to him in confession. Camisassa who did not become a bishop because he was *too* worthy to be one, and too valuable where he already was! The stuff that generals are made of, you bet! Yet this phenomenon of a man was an extraordinary model of humility and obedience.

Perhaps he also thought about this when Filippo Perlo left for Africa without saying goodbye. That was unkind of him — yes; but as rector he would have to put up with this. To practise patience and teach it to others. To know how to remain just and loving too towards someone who had insulted him in front of the whole Institute. And so indeed he did, for when the tittle-tattling echo against 'Kenya' (that is to say, against Bishop Perlo) reached him from the prefecture of Kafa, he did not hesitate for a moment to take the matter up with Fr Barlassina: 'If a stop were put to the antipathy and complaining that exist in certain quarters against Kenya, things would go a great deal better. . . And consider: you ought to be grateful to Kenya, if you are now being helped by us in your needs. . . Let us have no more of these troubles; shake hands like brothers.'

To Filippo Perlo of course, after that departure, he wrote immediately with a very specific list of mistakes that in his view were being made in the mission field, and with very precise instructions on how to remove the causes of discontent. Back came the bishop's reply at top speed: 'I beg Your Paternity to feel entirely free to give me definite orders in this respect; which, serving to lighten the responsibility from the exercise of which I neither can nor should exempt myself, will come to imprint on the work of my fellow-workers and myself in the mission field that uniformity to your wishes which perfectly represents my own most lively desire.'

Definite orders, uniformity of wishes: this is Filippo Perlo in his role as General, with his own peculiar vow of obedience. But why was there never any need for definite orders with his uncle? Who knows how often he ruminated over the contrast between them? But the moment came with brutal suddenness when he could only do so with hindsight. The year 1922 had been awaited as the year of the General Chapter, for the Institute's future to be assured. Instead it was first and foremost Giacomo Camisassa's last year on earth. The year of Joseph Allamano's bitterest blow.

The vice rector is no more

He had not fully recovered from an illness in 1919. The decline was visible. Fr Lorenzo Sales had been recalled from Africa to take over *La Consolata*, that most valuable of links between the missions and the faithful. And he certainly did not have time to spare for a document bearing the number 379926 and the date of 6 January 1920, issued by a German patent office: it concerned an invention of his, an exploit of Camisassa the engineer, who had taken it into his head after visiting Africa to invent a tractor for hilly places like those of their mission field. In fact his project for 'a tractor for sloping ground' came out and was first registered at the patent office in Turin and in Germany afterwards. Then the canon had to busy himself with other matters, letting the patent expire. Always in contact with him, Fr Sales described his illness like this: 'The colour of his face, the eyes as though veiled and the smile ever kind yet full of sadness, betrayed exhaustion and physical pain.'

We saw him busy over the Prefecture Apostolic of Iringa and in the summer of 1922 we still find him at work: negotiations in Rome, developments over the Chapter. . . For some time he had been tormented by nephritis and he spent the month of June at Rivoli, resting; then he returned to the Consolata. He alternated between desk and bed. Sometimes he would write a little. But less each time. On 19 July, signs of a stroke brought Allamano hurrying back to Turin from Sant'Ignazio. On 6 August, he still managed to say Mass. But after 10 August, there was a gradual capitulation to the illness, until the evening of 18 August when he was seen struggling to get out of bed, muttering that he had to go to the Institute. Those were his last words, his last actions. Allamano was present at the death-bed and recited the prayers for the dying. He did not have the strength to go to his funeral.

He wandered through the rooms of the Consolata, stopped in one: here we brought the Institute into being, here we took so many decisions, here we suffered too. . . Forty-two years, side by side, always devoted to each other, each with a huge respect for the other's opinions. Sometimes it was hard to say of a given idea, who had been its author; for Giacomo Camisassa was capable of enthusiastically and energetically support a given solution, having originally opposed it; in discussing the matter, they reached an understanding, and the positions from which they had set out were not important any more: 'Who is so wise that he knows all things? So do not place too much reliance on the rightness of your own views, but be ready to consider the views of others. If your opinion is sound, and you forgo it and follow that of another, you will win great merit. . .' (I, 9, 1). Yes, the *Imitation* again; it piloted them both, and no statistics exist to throw light on their reciprocal acts of renunciation. We only know about their total oneness in doing, once having discussed and decided together. On other occasions, they reached agreement without much discussion, because they had learnt to know each other, to foresee each other's reactions, inasmuch as 'it may even come about that each of two opinions is good.'

Explained in Joseph Allamano's own words, the reasons for this very lengthy attunement were basically two: 'If we achieved any good, it was precisely because we were so different; but we made a promise to tell each other the truth and we always kept it; if we had been equals, we should not have seen the faults in each other and should have made many more mistakes.'

In all correspondence, Giacomo Camisassa, when referring to Joseph Allamano, always addressed him 'Father' with a capital F. And it seems he actually pronounced it as a capital when speaking of him in the Institute or at the Consolata, when passing on his instructions. In public, he always spoke to him bareheaded, with his biretta in his hand. And if, on any special occasion, their chairs were placed side by side on a platform, he would be very quick to move his down and put himself on floor-level with everyone else.

When the rector went to Rome in the spring of 1919 for Fr Cafasso's cause, the vice rector immediately wrote to Fr Domenico Ferrero, the Institute's procurator in Rome, sending him a 'secret' letter about Joseph Allamano's diet and indicating what he liked best. In this letter to Fr Ferrero, Camisassa added: 'Be firm and insist that he eats his food, and keep me informed *every* day.'

It must have been appallingly hard for the rector to resume work without this daily meeting anymore. Particularly at a most delicate time: needs had increased in Africa, where from now on the three territories entrusted to the Institute would require twice as many staff; in Turin there were promising seminarians arriving and boys too for the junior seminary. But many other resources were needed which were not to be had; or at least not in Turin, but in Kenya under Bishop Perlo's charge. So, to requests for reinforcements, he was obliged to say, No. And to explain too to anyone in Turin who was anxious to leave: No surprise departure, no adventure. 'It's not the numbers that count when you are down there, it's the spirit that counts; and however great Africa's need may be, no individual is going to be sent there who has not first completed his or her training.'

But everything was more difficult now: coping with Bishop Perlo, following events in Kafa, keeping an eye on Iringa. And then for good measure to have some subordinate tell him that basically the Institute was not all that impressive when one considered that the Society of Jesus, during the lifetime of St Ignatius its founder, had already expanded on a far larger scale. So he needed to listen and reply to those unrealistic folk as well. But his fear was he would not be able to do it much longer. At seventy-one he was already one of the longest-lived of the Allamano family, and his frail health was now combined with the handicaps of old age.

In a word, it was absolutely essential to hurry everything up. The Missionary Institute could not be dependent on the probable illnesses of its founder. And then, this founder had a precise plan in mind: when the work of the Chapter was over, he would hand over his responsibilities and retire just to be rector of the Consolata and Pastoral Institute. And the Institute could stand on its own two feet. Few, very few founders have willingly given up the position, and he would be one of the very few. He had already decided on this with Giacomo Camisassa while the latter was still alive. His death was one more reason for not changing his mind.

So the next thing to be done was to nominate the delegates, or Chapter Fathers, to represent Mother House and the missions; and to take the opportunity of this for some of them to see Italy and their families again after being away so long. Then there were so many things to be decided. For instance: perhaps the time had come to give up the 'Piedmonticity' of the missionary priests and brothers. True, at the outset it had been a good thing, to start straight off from a small base of knowledge and shared assumptions, or, as Fr Gaudenzio Barlassina said: 'to succeed quicker in training its members into a single, compact body, uniting all our energies. Piedmont gave our Institute of its best, showing this region's generosity in the matter of adult subjects.' But for the present and future 'it would be important to recruit in the areas of Brescia, Padua, etc. and then one thing will lead to another.'

Yes, of course, this too shall be done. We ought to have thought of it before. Or better: the new governors of the Institute shall do it. As Giacomo Camisassa had said in April, in a letter to Fr Barlassina about the chapter: the Lord will see about missionaries; the Consolata will see about them, if the missionaries deserve it. He did not particularly like hearing himself called founder, even when there was no intent to flatter him. He turned it into a joke, saying that the Institute had a foundress, the Consolata (Our Lady of Consolation), and that he was more like a 'foundry-man', the fellow who ran through the money subscribed by people who supported the missions. In fact, as we have already said, he had 'melted down' his personal inheritance. His uncle Giovanni, the parish priest of Passerano, had left him a gold watch-chain and he gave this to the missions as well, using a length of cord instead. And so, he remarked with a smile, he had no more problems over making his will.

Naturally he prompted all his people to be equally

disinterested, repeating that one is no true missionary who does not practise self-mortification, that is to say, does not impose precise acts of renunciation on oneself and always stick to this. But he was rigorous, by way of contrast, over anything with a bearing on paying the blacks who worked in the Kenya farms and workshops. They must always be paid and paid regularly; not only for the obvious reason of justice, but because they had to be made aware of work as the means of improving their conditions. They had to understand that their hard work had a value and that this value could be converted into well-being, into a more acceptable life, into esteem, into growth for the whole family. He only saw the blacks in photographs and only heard them speak in letters, but few people of his day understood them as he had come to understand them, from his room in the Shrine of the Consolata in Turin.

12

The Superior General

'Chapter Fathers': a solemn title, but there were only twelve of them, meeting in a hall of the Pastoral Institute at the Consolata. Twelve, including Allamano: the little group that had carried the Institute's missionaries across continents. Bishop Filippo Perlo was invited too but had not come, and as bishop of somewhere else was under no obligation to take part.

In preparatory meetings they decided to accept the text of the Constitutions in the form Allamano had already presented to Propaganda Fide. They examined the general situation of the Institute and also drew up a Directory, or set of practical regulations for missionary work. And after a five-day break, the Chapter sessions proper began; there were to be two of them, 22 and 24 November 1922.

At the first, the business was to elect the Superior General of the Institute and his four councillors. And at the election of the former, the minutes record Joseph Allamano's suggestion that they should vote for somebody else: 'I cannot govern anymore; advancing years and failing strength make me physically and morally incapable of sustaining such a burden. It is a question of responsibility. I do not feel that I can assume it anymore. I had already decided with the late co-founder that we should both resign, for good, at the first chapter. . .'

When the votes were cast, eleven ballot papers out of twelve bore his name. And there was one vote for Bishop Perlo, which had obviously been cast by the rector. To his protests they replied that this was the Chapter's will; if they were to vote a hundred times over, the result would be the same. They then elected the councillors, of whom Filippo Perlo came out top by unanimous vote. Allamano proposed (subject to Propaganda Fide's approval, which was to come) that Perlo should be recognized as Vicar General with right of succession. At the session on 24 November, other community problems were examined and eventually the Chapter closed. Now the juridical establishing of the Institute within the framework of the universal Church was to take its course. As early as 27 February 1923, the Holy See approved the Constitutions '*ad decennium*' (for ten years).

(That same week, in the Palazzo Madama at Montecitorio, consistent majorities gave votes of confidence to the government formed by Benito Mussolini, Victor Emmanuel III having appointed him to succeed Luigi Facta. People thought of this as a normal change of government with a President of the Council born in Predappio replacing one born at Pinerolo; very few thought that a regime was round the corner.)

When the Chapter was over, there was a surprise from Africa! A telegram from Bishop Perlo: 'Cordial thanks for electing me. Very sorry have to refuse.' He did not want to be Vicar General, he did not want to leave Africa to take the job in Turin; and went back to insisting that more missionaries, more sisters, should be sent him. There was a copious and somewhat disagreeable exchange of correspondence between him and Allamano, and in the end Cardinal van Rossum, Prefect of Propaganda Fide, had to intervene. The latter ordered Filippo Perlo to lay down his charge as Vicar Apostolic of Kenya, to submit a list of possible successors (Propaganda Fide would make the choice) and to report to Turin and take up the post of Vicar General to which the Chapter of the Institute had summoned him. They did not have sight of him there however until the middle of 1924.

The year 1923 marked Agostino Richelmy's fifty years in the priesthood and his twenty-fifth year as bishop. For the Archbishop of Turin, these anniversaries were associated with the Piedmontese Regional Eucharistic Congress, held that spring. And, on 20 September, it would be fifty years in the priesthood for Joseph Allamano, too. To mark the occasion, a solemn celebration was to be held at the Consolata, with all those who had been ordained in 1873, the Cardinal among them. But Agostino Richelmy died after an operation on 10 August. After Giacomo Camisassa, Joseph Allamano had now lost this authoritative and cordial

164

landmark: the Cardinal whom he had always addressed on first name and who had always been ready with help, in Turin and in Rome.

'*Epularum adparatus. . . removeas*' ('Avoid sumptuous banquets'), Archbishop Gastaldi had recommended the new priests fifty years earlier. And at Castelnuovo that time it had been a very quiet affair. This time however things could not be limited to a little talk from the uncle-clergyman and a brother's doggerel verses. He received congratulations from hundreds of people of all walks of life, missionaries, generations of his pupils at the Pastoral Institutes; ten Cardinals wrote to him, among them his fellow-townsman Giovanni Cagliero. And the Pope in person, Pius XI, wrote him a long letter in his own hand, which began by praising his work at the Consolata: 'To you indeed. . . The Turinese ascribe the merit of not only having enlarged and, as it were, restored the Shrine from its foundations, but also of having taken every care in adorning it with works of art and covering its walls with richest marbles. . .' The letter went on to praise his work at the Pastoral Institute: 'It is wonderful how much and how hard you have worked to enrich the priests you have trained with doctrine and virtue. So it is that the priests can be numbered in hundreds and hundreds — among whom many bishops and archbishops — who rejoice in having been formed by you to a life worthy of the clergy.' Of the missions, Pius XI says: 'Such is the number of missionaries and of sisters who have already left for infidel lands and with such ardour do they discharge the exhausting duties of the apostolate, that your children, O beloved son, although arriving last in the field, do not seem to yield anything, either in little or much, to the veterans of other institutes.'

It was a document mightily reverberating from Rome to Turin, to Africa. But as regards its addressee, his famous 'lovely smile' must have faded progressively as he read the list of meritorious activities. Having taken it all in, at the end he could not help saying to a group of his seminarians: a bit of fun, yes, 'but no overstepping the mark please, as in the Pope's letter: I think they were trying to pull my leg. . .'

A handwritten letter from the Holy Father is always a

very fine thing. But what the Institute really prized was the news that arrived during the festivities for his Golden Jubilee: Propaganda Fide had definitely approved the Constitutions. Soon after was to come the civil recognition of the work as a non-profit-making charity.

'No overstepping the mark.' This also applied to the new missionary undertakings of the time. 'Doing good well' is only possible if the tasks and the resources are commensurate. Joseph Allamano was always faithful to the principle, even with Cesare Maria De Vecchi, a Piedmontese and member of the fascist 'quadrumvirate'. The latter visited Turin in October 1923 in his capacity as new governor of Somalia, being sent by Mussolini to rule that colony because there was not another one further away. Invited to De Vecchi's house, Allamano heard him propose the expansion of the Institute's missionary activity. The matter had been broached a number of times: it might be necessary to replace the Trinitarian Fathers down there. There were not many of them, and the governor did not like them anyway.

Allamano's answer was to suggest the new governor made a further attempt to reach agreement with the Trinitarians, since he did not like to have friction with other religious families. Furthermore he stressed that at the moment the Institute did not have any people ready. It would need time in any case, it would need money. . . In all, he did all he could to refuse politely.

'No overstepping the mark!' The Institute already had so many irons in the fire: Kenya, Kafa, Iringa, and so few missionaries. Not counting those who after so many years might want to come back to Italy; not counting those who would never come back again: like Fr Mario Botta of Saluzzo, missionary in Kafa, who died aged thirty in Addis Ababa in November 1923.

But a year had hardly gone by before, unexpectedly, the Institute accepted the Somalian mission. Propaganda Fide insisted it should do so, and had found one person instantly in agreement: Bishop Filippo Perlo, at last back from Africa in the spring of 1924, whom they interested in the matter during his visit to Rome in June-July. Thus, as early as 13 July, Joseph Allamano resigned himself to accepting, in a letter to Propaganda Fide where however he makes his motive very clear: 'Out of deference to the formal invitation addressed to me by that Sacred Congregation. . .' Be it known, in a word, that it was not what he wanted.

Fr Gabriele Perlo was to go and run the new enterprise; he was Bishop Filippo's brother and had twenty-one years of missionary experience behind him. He was to be Prefect Apostolic of Benadir; later he would be the first Vicar Apostolic of Mogadishu.

Here Allamano merely obeyed, and not without first telling the heads of Propaganda Fide in all sincerity how matters stood: 'very efficient' personnel had had to be taken from the Kenya Vicariate for the Kafa Prefecture, for the Iringa one and for the central directorate in Turin. Thus, all three territories were under-staffed. And it was impossible to reinforce them because in the Mother House 'there is only personnel in training'. Conclusion: for the time being, other missions could not be accepted. And the superior made matters clearer still: 'I said *for the time being*, since I hope that in two or three years' time the Institute will be better off for personnel. . .'

In two or three years' time! Once Somalia had been accepted, plans were made for expanding in other places. In the spring of 1925 negotiations began for sending Consolata missionaries to Mozambique as well; it was then under Portuguese rule and governed ecclesiastically speaking by a Portuguese bishop with the title of Prelate. Here penetration began in 1925 itself, having as first goal the region of the Zambesi. There were soon to be difficulties and quarrels, whether because of the number of missionaries arriving from Turin, or because they kept expanding their field of operations. Joseph Allamano however no longer played an active role in this and possibly was not fully informed about what was happening.

Filippo Perlo the cyclone

A scene change in Turin. From May 1924, the Archbishop was Giuseppe Gamba, sixty-six years old, a fellow-townsman of Joseph Allamano's (from San Damiano d'Asti) and above all his affectionate admirer. At the same time, Bishop Filippo Perlo was in Turin too: the Vicar General, given a festive welcome by all, beginning with the superior who was pleased to regard him as the best 'product' of the Institute in its as yet short history; as it were, a symbol of its dynamic, modern approach. He held you spell-bound by the vastness of his visions, backed by an extraordinary ability for getting things done; and his twenty years in Africa was a part of the family saga, with the British authorities, local chiefs, merchants and military, in war and peace. He had built workshops and factories, schools and seminaries and left a lively Christianity behind him with a rich future to come. And we ought to add here and now that Filippo Perlo's specific gifts as priest and bishop were also to be praised, after he had had to leave the Institute: 'a priest of greatest integrity, a most active apostle', 'great piety, edifying conduct in church', 'nothing to criticize about his priestly virtues or episcopal dignity'. Everyone agreed on this, even his critics.

A splendidly successful missionary therefore, whom however from now on we shall find all too often playing a saddening sort of anti-Allamano role. And we might be tempted to simplify: the struggle between good and evil, the meek and the arrogant, and so on with fault-finding, and so on with getting it wrong too. Here we should do better to let ourselves be informed and enlightened by Joseph Allamano, so as to get as clear a picture as we can of the times and manners in what it would seem right to define as an ordeal for the founder and his Institute, with all the difficulties and sorrows that were to form the raw material of its vigorous future.

Scarcely had he arrived, then, that in the internal newsletter *Da Casa Madre* Filippo Perlo was described, all in capital letters, as DUCE (leader); in other words, he was to 'write a new history'. Indeed, it seems that from this moment, and for some people in Mother House, there would be a *he* who was not Joseph Allamano. The latter in any case had always preferred to say 'we', never distinguishing between Giacomo Camisassa and himself.

Camisassa, too: Bishop Perlo's uncle, the much loved assistant rector. It was very surprising that, on his return to Turin, his nephew the Bishop had not at least celebrated a Mass for the repose of his soul. Indeed, to tell the truth, he had not been a single time to visit his tomb. Nothing. Allamano put up with this, saying nothing as long as he could. Then he acted in his tactful way, getting Sr Adelaide Marinoni to remind the Bishop about his uncle's anniversary, casually, suggesting a visit to the cemetery, a Mass. 'I did it,' Sr Adelaide recorded, 'using the very words the Father had put in my mouth, but they had no effect. How the Father suffered and perhaps even wept over the wrong done to the beloved assistant rector. . .'

But Joseph Allamano's room at the Consolata was not to become a weeping wall for those who did not care for Bishop Perlo's conduct of affairs. On the contrary, the rector lost no chance of speaking in his favour, showing that he very well appreciated the need for his presence and energy in the Institute. For instance, to a group of seminarians in 1925, he said: 'Always obey Bishop Perlo; love him; he is younger than I am and has more experience than I have in what the missions need. He will be able to develop the Institute further and make it livelier yet.'

Filippo Perlo had arrived in Turin with a strategy evidently thought-out well in advance, and he wasted no time. He began applying it at once, at the very roots, that is to say, with a new way of drumming up vocations. Nice talks with slides, an evening's excitement, were no longer enough. What were wanted were proper recruiting centres in every part of Italy: stable institutions staffed by people sent from Turin who would systematically stimulate interest by making contact with everybody in any way concerned (or who might become concerned) with missionary work. His activism aroused a new interest in missionary work throughout the Italian Catholic world. It was very effective too to publish information on the results, even the economic ones, achieved mainly in Kenya. He forwarded coffee from the mission farms to people all over the place; he took part with the Institute in the Rome International Missionary Exhibition of 1925; he also invented up-to-date ways of illustrating how evangelization was carried out. And vocations gradually began to increase. So much so that the Villa Lascaris, leased from the diocese at Pianezza, was no longer

169

big enough for the novitiate. And he boldly transferred everything to Sanfré in the province of Cuneo.

This last business is worth the following. Bishop Perlo bought the castle for 100,000 lire in June 1925 and there he installed the Institute's two novitiates, that of the missionaries and that of the sisters. Fast. Too fast. To convert the building he provided a few workmen, with the novices themselves. But in the first year, Fr Gallea recalled, 'Not only were there no conveniences but the water had to be drawn from a well more than 25 metres deep; we had to wait for the electricity company to lay on the light, and have recourse to stoves for heating.' The female novices had to wash the household linen in a ditch; instead of basins, they used empty tunny-fish tins. Sr Bianca Acquarone wrote: 'I think we suffered most from the intense cold, for the windows were in part draped with cloth and in part let the water in all over the place. Also the sanitary arrangements were rudimentary. . . and the clogs that gave us blisters on our heels.'

All in a rush and for the sake of missionaries-to-be. For the rest, it was typical of Filippo Perlo to believe that others were capable of the same austerities as he was; he had done this already in Africa. And it was certainly right to discourage future missionaries from being soft — Allamano said so too — but in that hurry to achieve, he often made serious mistakes: he began to neglect the work of religious formation, to push spirituality aside to some degree, to lay the stress on efficiency in a trade, on the rapid acquisition of technical skills. And since one thing leads to another, that growing demand for more personnel to take over more missions led fatally to the worst of expedients: an enforced shortening of the time for ordination.

Between the two of them, in other circumstances, there could have been a difference in method, different ways of achieving the same object. But for Allamano, speedy ordination was not another way; it was unacceptable. For him there could not be such a thing as a good missionary who was not a good priest, completely formed in the regular itinerary of studies and preparation. In this field, urgency was not what counted. This was also true of course for the sisters; he would never approve of their being sent out to the mission field the moment they had finished their novitiate.

Over the Consolata Missionary Sisters there was a further reason for radical disagreement between the two men. As founder, Joseph Allamano was the natural superior of the female community as well. But for the future, he saw an evolution similar to that of other mixed religious families — where the sisters develop to autonomy, to their 'coming of age', while still retaining shared aims. Filippo Perlo however seems to have seen the missionary troops of the Consolata (priests, brothers, sisters) more or less as three battalions of a regiment commanded by one colonel, with the sisters regarded as an under-age auxiliary unit, now and forever.

It was not to turn out like this, but years would go by and Joseph Allamano would not be alive to see it. What he did see then and there was an ensemble of schemes that Filippo Perlo was bringing to fruition on several fronts — always energetically, even brilliantly, but with one capital defect: haste. He wanted to do things in three to four years that needed at least ten. To do this, in certain cases, involves the disadvantages of Sanfré, with a big house with no electricity and many of the windows with no glass in them; but here at least it is possible to repair it and put it in order. With people, however, to skip these years is fatal. Especially with regard to the studies and training of priests and religious. They may learn to do without central heating in an old castle, but their years of studying, no, these cannot be abridged, nor can they be replaced or improvised. One of the novice masters, a future bishop, Giuseppe Nepote-Fus, noted, 'studies reduced, teaching neglected, regulations set aside', contrary to Joseph Allamano's orders, owing to 'the excessive stress laid on manual work'. And here we are, the old rector might think, in danger of entrusting the Gospel to ignorant priests, 'images of sadness and disappointment, for the anger of God and the desolation of the people.'

All this was further aggravated by the nature of the relationship between the old man and the young one, as well as by the absence of rapport. The former admired the splendid qualities of the latter and had deep respect for his dignity as bishop. And the latter had not lost his veneration for the founder. But they could not confide in each other. Neither of them could unburden himself to the other; they did not discuss for hours, as in Giacomo Camisassa's days. Then certain impetuous things Bishop Perlo did in all good faith, and certain misunderstandings, would account for the rest. They were never to be friends anymore.

The heroism of silence

With Camisassa, he had intended to retire from the Missionary Institute on reaching a certain age. To stay at the Consolata and look after the Pastoral Institute would have been enough. Now however, with these changes, he could indeed have gone away, after a solemn leave-taking as founder, staying outside as a sort of oracle without responsibilities or problems. Yet he stayed on. Particularly now, with so many new things and not all of them, in his opinion, good. From now on, other people were to be the ones to do things and tell him afterwards. Each day brought new bitterness, new disillusion; his old age was not to know the satisfactions that other founders may have enjoyed.

Perhaps it was precisely because of this that Joseph Allamano remained at his post: to offer his suffering as a service to his missionaries of the day and of the days to come. In other words, to go on working at their training. He did not often give talks anymore, not all that many decisions passed through his hands; but his silence too was very useful in moulding souls, one by one; that was how he taught. Through the years he had gone on making notes and jotting down examples in order to teach them all the value of obedience. And now he himself was the example; not saying a word, he taught how to obey, not so much individual superiors who come and go, as the spirit of the Institute itself. The fact that he remained at its head even in such conditions was encouraging for everyone, whatever they might think about the novelties introduced by Perlo's management.

One might have called him a victim, at certain moments. But he was not. He remained the teacher, and was also a witness. Remaining at his post although deprived of power

172

was not passive endurance on his part but an active decision. He thought he was needed. He knew himself to be, more than anyone, the one who guaranteed the persistence — hidden as it might be like a seed in the soil — of the spirit which had given life to this missionary family. It was for him, with his physical presence, to show faith in the secure future of the Institute as a work willed by God and hence also summoned to many ordeals and crosses, but always with all the vigour needed for overcoming them.

As one of his successors, Fr Gaudenzio Barlassina, bore witness: 'He suffered very much towards the end of his life, when — as I heard him say in community — he was no longer consulted as formerly. He showed no resentment however and bore this ordeal with great fortitude and charity.'

'Little by little,' says Bishop Nepote-Fus, 'he was pushed to one side, as someone to be respected and trotted out on solemn and gala occasions.' It was like a succession of pushes, more or less perceptible, one after another; but with the result that he found himself out of the Institute although he was still its superior. Not indeed that he was not loved or that his merits went unrecognized. But all that belonged to the past. The present was made up of other things, other programmes, another average per hour, another casualness. Very concisely, Fr Candido Bona depicts the new situation: 'Certainly there was no diminishing of Bishop Perlo's formal respect. Nor perhaps of his interior respect. But the founder must have seemed to him a venerable wreck.'

And his non-interference might indeed have seemed like the resigned acceptance of an old man by this time sinking into apathy. But the effect of it was that he suffered acutely. He found the situation very painful; he was far from apathetic. But plainly he was helped by knowing that he was fulfilling a duty and by his native capacity for self-control, as Sr Chiara Strapazzon observed: 'Even during this ordeal, I never saw him disturbed; much in pain, yes, but always calm and tranquil. I never heard a word of resentment against the person who had been the cause of it. Only, talking to me, he sometimes used to say: "Those people over there (the missionaries) do not need me anymore, but you still need me." '

173

The man who, faced with a very solemn eulogy from the Pope, could observe that someone must have been pulling his leg (i.e., suggesting such compliments), knew how to draw on his own weakness for teaching material. Once it happened that he got angry on surprising the sisters in the Mother House eating ices. They explained to him they had been working very hard and the ice-cream was a little reward given them by Bishop Perlo (him already; but during his visit in 1921). 'He got angrier still,' Sr Ambrosina Riccardi recalled, 'and then he said that the spirit (of the rule) should be taken from him, not from the bishop. But the next day they saw him come back, pale and upset; 'He knelt down, made the sign of the cross, gazed at the image of the Consolata. Then he said: "I have come to ask pardon for my act of impatience yesterday. I was quick-tempered." He went on to say other things I cannot really remember, but tending to stress that he had unjustifiably lost his temper. . . Before going out, he again asked our pardon and then blessed us. When he said: "I ask your pardon again, don't follow my bad example, and now I give you my blessing," we all burst out crying.'

'I shall have to speak up from heaven!' This was a witticism of his, quoted by more than one witness, as a catch-phrase, a good-natured threat at the things that most displeased him in community. Given that this used to happen only a few years before he died, the words may have taken on a prophetic tinge. But they have a precise significance in the story as further proof of the quality of his silences: they were not giving-in, not capitulation, not old age. They were meant. Still and always they had a formative purpose, and that intermittent flashing of plans 'from heaven' taught his listeners precisely not to misconstrue him.

In August 1923, for him, the very long-standing custom of the retreat at Sant'Ignazio came to an end. Those meetings with priests from all over the place, those reunions with former pupils from the Pastoral Institute, those summers of memories and plans, with the joyful greetings for those arriving and the sad farewells, with the coffee he always made a point of having ready for every new arrival, in a word that deep feeling of being a father: that was all over. Some of his old pupils were dead already; some of them were now ailing bishops. And he, in his seventies, is himself no longer fit enough to go back to those altitudes. He has a sort of pact with the doctors: they will help him to live long enough to see Giuseppe Cafasso beatified. And so he must do what they say: plenty of rest, plenty of time in bed, no more Lanzo Valleys.

He bade farewell to those fifty years and more of his life, Fr Sales relates, in his intense, meek way. He prayed long, stopping at each altar in the church (raised by the Jesuits in the eighteenth century to replace the seventeenth century chapel built by the inhabitants of Mezzenile). And he made a longer stop of course before the altar of St Ignatius. What numbers of people have passed this way, coming from all over Piedmont in the long history of retreats; and what great retreat leaders, such as Pio Brunone Lanteri, to name one of them! Now he, Canon Allamano counts as one of the front-ranking personages in this history; but in the August of 1923 he was able to step down with total absence of ceremony.

It became more and more difficult for him to go to Mother House even to say good-bye. And he did not like the new style in which the missionaries left, under Bishop Perlo's direction. The aim was probably good and to some extent anticipated the days of total communication: besides getting things done, thought the bishop from Kenya, things must be seen to be getting done. And a resounding departure of missionaries cannot but benefit the missions by way of financial help and even perhaps new vocations.

Filippo Perlo may well have been right. But Joseph Allamano was never to be converted to noise, even the best intentioned. It was humility with its very close kinsman called good taste; and above all, trust in something different from public relations and the policy of the public image. And when he thinks that among the new missionaries there are eager lads quickly accepted and swiftly sent far away. . .
When he does happen to speak at the Institute, he is not ashamed of repeating himself, as in October 1924: 'Be few! We do not have a mania for having much land (that is to say, much mission territory) and we do not have the hands to work it; better few missions but well looked after. . . May the Lord send others! But only first class stuff! That's what

175

I want. . . Each of us ought to be able to do the work of many others. . .'

He was now seventy-three, his legs were swollen and the doctors' orders were bed and easy-chair, but he was ever himself: 'Only first class stuff.'

Fr Tubaldo noted that 'there was something very important he wanted to do before he died: he left Bishop Perlo a message of reproof which was to be delivered after his death; he spoke to many members of the Institute besides; he clearly expressed his thought, his anxieties, his sufferings. . . as though depositing in their souls *the seeds of his spirit*, which when the time was ripe would germinate.'

13

Uncle Giuseppe among the Blessed

Allamano usually went from the Consolata to Mother House by tram. On one occasion we hear tell of a carriage, and it is the kind of story one would prefer not to hear. It was told by Canon Giuseppe Cappella while his successor at the Consolata, and must go back to the late summer of 1925. Anyhow, it was a Sunday. The Superior General had been visiting Mother House to attend some speeches in his honour. He then began, as was his wont, to go round the Institute and have a word with everyone. But at that moment the superior of the house told him the carriage was waiting for him. 'It was,' said Canon Cappella, 'obviously a way of getting rid of him. Allamano did not say a word, climbed into the carriage and came back to the Shrine. I saw him come into the sacristy rather downcast and his left eye looking very inflamed. I ran towards him. . . I asked him where he had been and what had happened to him. He replied that he had come from the Institute, and added: "They do not want me anymore. They do not want me anymore. Let them do as they please, provided they act according to the spirit of the rule. . ." Then he prayed for a long time, and shortly afterwards came in to supper without showing the slightest resentment.'

That the invitation to get in the carriage was a way of quickly getting him out of the Institute remains to be proved; but here is not the place to put others on trial. He is the one we are interested in. And he, look how he reacts: from the 'they do not want me anymore' to his serene arrival at the supper table, having prayed. In the same manner we may perhaps treat of another incident, almost at the end of his life: when the bill reached him from Mother House for the Kenya coffee which he often received for his own use and for giving as presents. In this case, this was attributable to an order of Bishop Perlo

177

but interpreted in such a way as wronged the man who was perhaps capable of big mistakes but not of this pettymindedness. Bishop Perlo, as we have already said, was also very keen on administration and insisted on the proper keeping of accounts. It was natural therefore that he should want precise and prompt payment for the coffee sent to various destinations. And some obedient and obtuse servant (the scourge of centralized governments) seems to have disastrously misunderstood. The result: Giuseppe Allamano could also imagine that he was being asked to account for all the cups of coffee he had sipped and the little packets he had presented to this benefactor or the other; all this in the name of the Missionary Institute of which he was the Superior General, and for which he had given all his personal property, even down to the watch-chain left him by his uncle the parish priest.

We do not know how this story actually ended, nor what Joseph Allamano had actually thought about it. We do however know that a few days after the incident (and after many other incidents), his seventy-fifth birthday occurred. And to mark the occasion and break with the habits of a lifetime, he invited Bishop Perlo and Fr Giuseppe Gallea, the Bursar General, to lunch. He welcomed them — this old man who gets stronger the older he grows — with his 'lovely smile' for festive occasions.

All the more so because, in the meantime, an event had occurred that had taken up a great part of his life: the beatification of his uncle Giuseppe Cafasso.

From 1921 to 1924, those in charge of the causes of the saints had been keeping him constantly informed about progress made, 'decisive' steps concluded, each of these 'opening the way' to other phases, to other moments, rites and proceedings of the *iter* henceforward. And the day came on which the story might be said at last to have ended: on 1 January 1925, Joseph Allamano learned that the date for the beatification had been fixed for 3 May the same year.

From that instant onwards, his obedience to the doctors was total: 'To save up a bit of strength, I never dare go out of doors. . . I shall go to Rome. . .'

And with him to Rome, at his own expense, he takes all the students of the Pastoral Institute, some thirty in all. Joseph Cafasso's beatification is a feast-day for them too.

At Rome he is the guest of the Salesians headed by Cardinal Cagliero, and takes part in the whole long, tiring succession of ceremonies. Canon Nicola Baravalle noted: 'The day of the beatification was immensely tiring for him with his precarious health. However he took part in the morning service and then in the afternoon one as though transfigured, without any hint of tiredness or strain. . . In the afternoon, at the papal service, I was near him and tried to catch his attention, but he barely replied, preferring a state of recollection in which his frail person seemed totally absorbed.'

We see him back in Turin at the diocesan celebrations. The climax occurred on 21 June when Giuseppe Cafasso's remains were carried into the Shrine of the Consolata, with Archbishop Gamba and other Piedmontese bishops. Canon Baravalle noted: 'He was the nearest relative to the Blessed, the promoter of the cause, the superior of the Shrine and the Pastoral Institute, and people expected to see him proceed in glory, wearing full canonicals, to a special seat. Instead, he came with us of the Shrine behind the sacred relics, just wearing his cassock and carrying a lighted torch. . . He dragged himself along so painfully that at one point he had to lean on his torch and I was worried he was going to faint. . .'

The year 1925 passed partly in waiting for and partly in the fulfilment of the great events in Rome and Turin concerning Giuseppe Cafasso. And he referred to him as 'your uncle' even to the Consolata missionaries. This was not the exaltation of a kinsman, pursued through thirty years of negotiation, effort and expense. He had wanted to complete the undertaking as a sign of his love for the Church. A love taking concrete form in his total devotion to a single ideal: the Catholic clergy and its holiness, which was to be cultivated at every moment, in every place, in the parish and in the mission field, to be increased by examples and glorified in its greatest masters. All this was stupendously served by the brief life of Giuseppe Cafasso, the priest of the Pastoral Institute and of the gallows, exalted by the entire Catholic community and held up as a model and point of reference.

Now he could truly let go. This little seventy-fifth birthday luncheon party with Bishop Perlo and Fr Gallea: what a gesture, what a high moment of the Allamano style, or indeed of elegant charity! A few days later however the twenty-fifth anniversary of the Institute came round, founded by him, Joseph Allamano in that now vanished Turin of long ago. It seems no one remembered him: no ceremonies, no party, not even the usual speeches.

Joseph Allamano spent the day copying out his will: the fifth and last one: 'I leave whatever I possess at my death of real and personal property to the Reverend Canon Giuseppe Cappella, Vice Rector and Sacristy Prefect in the Shrine of the Consolata and to the Reverend Father Giuseppe Gallea, Consolata Missionary born in Revigliasco.' The heirs in previous wills had been named as Bishop Perlo and Fr Gays. Now, however, we have one heir belonging to the Consolata and the other to the Institute. Fr Candido Bona observes: 'In a certain sense this is a return to beginnings. The founder, who in the course of the last two decades had made over virtually his entire and large estate to the Institute, did not belong, juridically at least, to the work of which he was the superior. He was still a diocesan priest.' And the diocesan ideal had been the passion of his life, year after year, bishop after bishop. To the Institute, besides that portion of his property, he left this brief and marvellous message: 'For you, my dear missionaries and missionary sisters, I have lived all these years and for you I have used up possessions, health and life. I hope in dying to become your protector in heaven.'

The last Mass

On Sunday 31 January 1926, some of the sisters came to see him at the Consolata. He was tired, his voice even fainter than usual; his legs were swollen and he had trouble breathing. He hoped to be able to say Mass until the last day of his life. But the last Mass was to be the one on 1 February. He tried once or twice to get up, but that was it. From then on, he was never left alone. He spoke with growing difficulty and often, for long periods, remained wrapped in prayer. Alarm set in on 11 February and in the Consolata Archbishop Gamba took part in a *triduum* of prayer for his recovery. On 13 February, the invalid insisted on seeing Mgr Perrachon, bishop-elect of Nyeri in Kenya: he knew he had arrived in Turin, had him summoned and they conversed. He was the second of 'his Bishops'.

'Oh, Father. This is it. You are dying on me,' Sr Emerenziana Tealdi exclaimed on the morning of 15 February, on coming back into his room and finding that he had got worse in a matter of minutes. He still managed to answer: 'And you pray that God's will be done.' In the afternoon, students of the Pastoral Institute, missionaries and sisters filed into his room, escorting the Body of Christ which was administered to him in the form of Viaticum, Archbishop Gamba with the two Bishops Perlo and Perrachon being present. Filippo Perlo then asked him for his last blessing for all the missionaries in Turin and Africa. He made a sign of assent and tried to raise his hand, which however fell back inert. He blessed them with his eyes and soul. Finally the death agony began, which lasted for twelve hours, ending at 4.10 a.m. on 16 February 1926. Sr Emerenziana Tealdi stated: 'At about three o'clock at night, his appearance suddenly changed; his face lit up, a smile appeared on his lips, his eye became clear, gazing fixedly into the distance. I called to him: "Father!" He understood and turned his eyes towards me and gazed at me. It was the last look he gave on earth; he expired shortly afterwards. When the vice rector (Camisassa) died, I had felt very much afraid; but at the rector's death I felt a great, inexplicable peace in my soul.'

Bishop Filippo Perlo described his end as follows: 'He remained lucid right to the last; he responded to the prayers for the dying which were being said around him. And without any struggle he serenely expired in the early hours of the morning of 16 February 1926. His death was so peaceful that those present were barely aware it had happened and had to wait a little while before being sure he was dead.'

On 18 February, thousands of Turinese attended Canon Allamano's last journey to the cathedral, along the same route he had followed for forty years. First of all, the Consolata clergy made their farewells in the Shrine, the students of the Pastoral Institute being there too. In the cathedral, the Church of Turin paid its respects to its priest, Joseph Allamano. The body was eventually taken to the general cemetery to be buried close to Giacomo Camisassa. But this was to be only temporary. It was already being said on the very day of the funeral that the canon would be making another journey in the opposite direction. And so it proved: in 1938 his remains were translated, by way of the Consolata, to the Mother House of the missionaries.

And he has remained there ever since, in the Missionary Institute in Corso Ferrucci, daily repeating his advice to all who devote their lives to spreading the Gospel: 'The missionary's holiness must be something special. My words may perhaps make an impression on you or even bewilder some of you. Well, that cannot be helped. What I say is for those who desire to acquire the holiness proper to a missionary. . . Holiness is one, but varied is the form and differing are the ways to attain it. In the community I see a holiness too commonplace. The Lord who inspired this foundation has also inspired the necessary ways and means of achieving perfection and making yourselves saints.'

So, from his death until now, Joseph Allamano has never left his missionaries in peace, by holding out this hardest of ideals: 'In a missionary, one must be able to see God.' So conciliatory with everyone, so ready to understand, justify and forgive so many things directed against himself by making allowance at least for a good intention, in matters of evangelization this man made allowances for nobody, offered no negotiable prices: 'Only first class people.'

Now, *his* Christians, coming from every part of the world, raised up by him by means of the missionaries, gather round the man who lived his entire existence in silence and who never once set foot outside Italy. Young churches come, which we might almost call native to Turin, by way of Corso Ferrucci and the Consolata, since he it was who dreamed of them and first thought about them when assembling, training and sending forth the first group of evangelizers: young churches with their own bishops, their own priests and faithful, heirs to the teaching of those first splendid black catechists, Christians of the first water.

In his will, Joseph Allamano left a thousand lire each to the nursery school and the hospital of Castelnuovo d'Asti. He had often sent money presents to institutions and individuals. Throughout her life, his 'official' almoner had been his school-teacher Benedetta Savio. Later he had attended to this himself, through relatives. And he made his last farewell to Castelnuovo in September 1925, a few months before his death. There were celebrations for Cafasso's beatification; a new altar in the parish church had been dedicated in his honour, also with money contributed by Joseph Allamano (even 'almost totally donated', according to his niece Pia Clotilde Allamano).

During that stay, he had made a point of saying Mass in a chapel dedicated to the Consolata, where as a young priest fifty-two years before he had been to say one of his first Masses. And all the memories of the olden days came flooding back: of Fr Rossi the parish priest; of Fr Giovanni Allamano his uncle; of the signs worked by Don Bosco, still alive; of the fame and dramas attending Fr Bertagna. And of his mother Marianna Allamano Cafasso during her years of illness: in those Septembers when he was on holiday to read to her, now she was blind, and in the end to converse with her by patting her hand in that loving code of theirs. . . Like a long review of the dead, this last visit. But without any sadness, since memory brought simple, noble beings to life again, men and women 'of the first water' among those rugged hills.

Pia Clotilde Allamano relates one of the last moments of Joseph Allamano's last stay in Castelnuovo d'Asti as follows: 'Being one morning on the terrace of my house where one enjoys, as part of the magnificent panorama, a view of the cemetery, Canon Allamano, seeing this, immediately thought of the dead. . . He was sitting on an upright chair. He stood up and, bareheaded, recited the *De profundis* and the *Oremus*, while I was kneeling beside him, moved by the evocation of dear memories.'